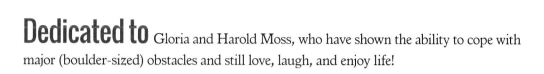
Dedicated to Gloria and Harold Moss, who have shown the ability to cope with major (boulder-sized) obstacles and still love, laugh, and enjoy life!

Inspired by Scott Moss, who as a teenager, found out that he had cancer and strived to be resilient as he faced this obstacle. For example, when he learned that he would lose his hair temporarily due to the treatment that he needed, he bought and proudly displayed a sticker that read: "Bald is Beautiful." He lived by the well-known quote, "When life gives you lemons, make lemonade," and he strived to live each moment to the fullest, while also being realistic and responsible about facing his situation. Scott knew that he could either make the best of the situation or he could focus on the illness and treatment side effects, and stop doing things he had enjoyed prior to getting cancer. He made the courageous move to be resilient!

BOUNCE BACK

how to be a resilient kid

by Wendy L. Moss, PhD

MAGINATION PRESS · WASHINGTON, DC · AMERICAN PSYCHOLOGICAL ASSOCIATION

Published by MAGINATION PRESS®
An Educational Publishing Foundation Book
American Psychological Association, 750 First Street NE, Washington, DC 20002

Magination Press is a registered trademark of the American Psychological Association.

For more information about our books, including a complete catalog, please write to us, call 1-800-374-2721, or visit our website at www.apa.org/pubs/magination.

Book design by *Hunt Smith Design*

Printed by Worzalla, Stevens Point, WI

LIBRARY OF CONGRESS CATALOGING-IN-PUBLICATION DATA
Moss, Wendy (Wendy L.)
 Bounce back : how to be a resilient kid / by Wendy L. Moss.
  pages cm
 ISBN 978-1-4338-1921-6 (hardcover) — ISBN 1-4338-1921-X (hardcover) — ISBN 978-1-4338-1922-3 (pbk.) — ISBN 1-4338-1922-8 (pbk.) 1. Resilience (Personality trait)—Juvenile literature. 2. Resilience (Personality trait) in children—Juvenile literature. I. Title.

 BF723.R46M67 2016

 155.4'1824—dc23   2014046875

Manufactured in the United States of America
First printing March 2015
10 9 8 7 6 5 4 3 2 1

Contents

1 What Is Resilience?   7

2 Getting to Know Yourself Better   11

3 Understanding Emotions   21

4 Using Self-Talk   33

5 Calming Yourself   43

6 Handling Decisions, Disappointments, and New Challenges   53

7 Having the Power of Change   63

8 Dealing With Social Conflicts   73

9 Coping With Unchangeable Situations   87

10 Building a Support Team   101

Conclusion: Don't Stop! Your Resiliency Journey Continues   109

About the Author   111

About Magination Press   112

CHAPTER ONE

What Is Resilience?

Everyone faces challenges at some point during their lives. Some of these experiences may be negative or unpleasant, like dealing with a serious illness, being lonely, getting a low grade on a test, fighting with a sibling, or not getting selected for a team. Some positive experiences can create stress, too. For example, imagine you are offered the chance to swim on the varsity swim team at your school. You might be excited for the opportunity, but also feel stressed at the same time—perhaps you would wonder if you were talented enough, or worry about the hard work that would be required. How would you cope with this stress? Would you withdraw from the team because of self-doubts and anxiety or would you have the coping strategies to deal with your emotions and enjoy the new opportunity?

Take a moment to think about what is creating stress in your own life. Are you struggling with a difficult subject in school, a conflict with a friend, or another uncomfortable or stressful situation? If so, how do you handle it? Do you have strategies for getting through these tough times? Have you ever heard the saying "When life gives you lemons, make lemonade"? It means that even when something doesn't go the way you would want or you are facing a very stressful experience, there are ways to cope with it and make the best of the situation. A resilient person can often do this. As you become more resilient, you may find that you are better able to do this too!

What Does It Mean to Be Resilient?

Resilience is like a bouncing ball. When the ball hits the ground, we expect it to bounce back. Resilience means you can bounce back from, or deal with, difficult times, new situations, unexpected changes, or other experiences that cause you stress.

Keep in mind that being resilient does not mean that you don't feel pain or that everything goes your way. Actually, you are more resilient after going through a stressful situation and learning to deal with the challenge or setback. If you find ways to handle difficult situations today, you are likely to feel more confident that you can handle future tough times without feeling totally overwhelmed.

How This Book Can Help

Some people seem to just bounce back automatically—they understand how to be resilient. However, resilience is not something you are born with or not—it can be learned. If two people face the same obstacles, the person who is resilient will often feel less stress than the person who is not resilient. Resilient people learn ways to work around or overcome stresses.

In this book, you will learn strategies for how to be resilient more often and more easily. There are three major steps toward becoming resilient:

step one Know yourself and what makes you happy or stressed.

step two Learn strategies to help you get through the stressful times.

step three Use these strategies in your life.

The chapters that follow cover these steps and help you gain the important life skill of resilience. You will learn how to figure out whether a stressful situation is within your power to change, and then how to accept, adapt, or change the situation. You will read about when to tackle a problem on your own and when to ask for advice or support. Plus, you will read about how self-talk, calming techniques, and other specific strategies for dealing with conflicts and challenges can build resilience and prepare you for life's roadblocks, obstacles, and challenges that you may face in future years.

You will read a lot about how other kids found ways to bounce back from stressful times. However, in order to protect the privacy of all of the children and teens who have shared their stories, the examples are composites and describe many kids. These examples are not meant to reveal the challenges faced by an individual person.

So, do you want to get "unstuck" from worry, anger, sadness, or general stress? Do you want to gain confidence that you can handle challenges because you have coping strategies for bouncing back? Do you want to learn ways to deal with uncomfortable times so that you aren't super down about them? If you answered "yes" to any of these questions, then it sounds like you would benefit from finding a way to become resilient. Being motivated to learn resiliency skills is a great first step toward acquiring them! This book will offer you tons of tips that you can use to help you to reach your resiliency goals!

CHAPTER TWO

Getting to Know Yourself Better

How well do you know yourself? Do you know what stresses you out, what you feel at different times and during different activities in your day, and how to calm yourself even when you are nervous, angry, upset, or overwhelmed? You might think that you know yourself pretty well, since you are with yourself 24 hours a day, every day of your life! The truth is that you probably don't spend much time thinking about what you feel, why you react the way you do, and what strategies you use to deal with stress. That's okay.

This chapter will challenge you to become a detective and figure out what your "stress triggers" are, what stresses you out, and how you react to stress. You will get a chance to learn more about *you*. Remember the three steps towards becoming more resilient, from Chapter One? Learning about yourself is the first step!

Before reading this chapter, take a minute to think more about you:

When I am tense, upset, or stressed, I

a) don't know what to do

b) hope that other people notice that I am stressed and help me

c) have some "go-to" people and some relaxing activities that usually help me calm down and feel happier

I am eating lunch with my friends, but become distracted and feel my muscles tense. I

a) don't usually think about or notice this stuff

b) notice that I'm distracted and tense, but I'm not sure why

c) realize that I'm stressed and know why, like when I'm nervous about a test in my class the next period

When I am stressed—whether I am at a party, studying, or doing something else—I

a) have no idea how I act when I am stressed

b) might shake my leg or look away from people, but I don't notice these things unless someone points them out to me

c) know when I'm stressed and how I act when I am stressed

When I'm upset, overwhelmed, or tense, I

a) keep my emotions private and don't tell anyone

b) want to share my emotions with people I trust, but am not sure what to say

c) know how to communicate my emotions to people I trust

Sometimes certain situations can trigger stress. I

a) don't know what my "stress triggers" are

b) know what will trigger stress sometimes but can't often predict when it will happen

c) know some common situations that will make me stressed, so in those situations I try to find ways to relax and not get tense

If you answered mostly "a": You are still learning about yourself and what makes you stressed. You will likely benefit greatly from key tools that you will read about soon in this book!

If you answered mostly "b": You are well on your way to understanding yourself, but might benefit from learning more about your stress triggers.

If you answered mostly "c": You have a good understanding of what causes you stress. Additional tools to calm yourself and deal with stress might be helpful for you.

What Makes You Happy?

Take a moment to think about what makes you happy. What are some activities you like to do? Which friends do you like talking to? What skills or qualities do you have that you take pride in? How do you entertain yourself? What makes you comfortable? What do you enjoy about yourself?

Just knowing how you play, think, act, or behave is powerful stuff. This information can allow you to learn what you can do, or what you can think about, to help you to relax and feel less stress. So, on a separate sheet of paper, take a minute to write down what activities and thoughts make you happy. Review this list whenever you want to help yourself to relax, calm down, and ultimately get "unstuck" when you are stuck!

Seven Questions to Ask Yourself

Next, think about what causes you stress. Try to figure out what's going on in your thoughts, feelings, and actions. To help you figure out the cause of your stress and how you cope, it can be helpful to ask yourself the questions below.

❶ Can you recognize when you are stressed? Or do you wait for someone else to comment about how you seem "moody" or "angry" or different in some way?

❷ Can you figure out why you are stressed? Can you easily finish this sentence: "I am stressed out because…"?

❸ What are your stress triggers? That is, what situations happen over and over that keep stressing you out?

❹ Does your stress ruin good times? Does the difficult situation cause you to be so upset that you really can't enjoy the fun times?

❺ Can you name your emotions when you feel uneasy?

❻ How do other kids handle the situation that makes you uncomfortable?

❼ What strategies can you use? What can you do to deal with the stress in your life?

Now, let's investigate and think about your answers through the next several sections. Time to solve this mystery and get to know yourself better!

DID YOU KNOW?

Having an awareness of your emotions and thoughts can be an important step toward developing resiliency skills. Researchers have found that as children spend time enjoying experiences, they may learn more about their feelings and healthy ways to deal with them. Plus, they can even learn ways to regulate their emotions and cope with difficult challenges. In other words, they become more resilient. So enjoy what you are doing! It can help you be resilient!

Coholic, D.A. (2011). Exploring the feasibility and benefits of arts-based mindfulness-based practices with young people in need: Aiming to improve aspects of self-awareness and resilience. *Child Youth Care Forum, 40,* 303–317.

❶ Can You Recognize When You Are Stressed?

Once you understand yourself well, it becomes easier to recognize the signs that you are stressed. First, think about a time when you experienced a really strong emotion that doesn't typically happen on a regular day. For example, maybe you were relieved about finishing a test, happy about an upcoming vacation, or upset because your favorite basketball team lost a game. There's no right or wrong answer. It's just helpful to think about how you feel when you are experiencing emotions different from your "baseline" on a typical day. But how can you tell if you are stressed? There are definitely some behaviors you might do when you are stressed that can be a clue that you are uncomfortable or upset. For example, do you feel tense in your body, like you want to punch your pillow? Do you get easily annoyed at other people? Do you eat a lot? Do you hide in your room and feel down?

Some common signs of stress include:

- a change in your sleep habits—sleeping more or less than you normally do
- a change in diet—eating more or less or different food than you normally would
- having less or more energy
- feeling misunderstood

- having trouble concentrating
- crying or yelling a lot
- a change in your overall mood

Recognizing these behavior clues can help you work backward and figure out what caused you to be stressed in the first place.

If you aren't aware of how you react when stressed, ask people who know you well, like your parent, best friend, or even a trusted teacher. Ask them to let you know what they notice when you are stressed. Erica's teacher said that she frequently noticed that Erica seemed to chew on her lower lip when she was nervous about an upcoming test. Erica hadn't known this about herself. Frequently, kids and adults communicate through their body language, in addition to words. What secrets do you share through your own body language?

Everyone shows or feels stress differently. What's important is to figure out how you experience stress. Once you notice the signs that you are stressed, you'll be able to take steps to deal with it—and that's an important tool to have as you become resilient!

❷ Can You Figure out Why You Are Stressed?

Did you know that there are different kinds of stress? Your stress can be external, internal, or both. *External stress* is stress that happens because of situations around you. For example, imagine that you turn on the television and learn that there is a war going on in another part of the world. You can't stop the war, but you can become stressed by the violence and destruction it is causing. This external stress might cause you to become afraid or anxious. You might get angry because you are disappointed in the human race or be short-tempered with those around you. These are all signs that you are stressed.

Internal stress is stress that occurs from your own thoughts and behaviors, and you have a lot of control over it. It is stress that comes from inside you. For example, if you expect to be perfect and then become angry at yourself when you receive a high but not perfect grade, this is internal stress.

There are lots of situations that can lead to both internal and external stress. For example, imagine that you are upset because you didn't receive an award at the end of the school year for attending your school's before-school peer mentoring program. Your friends who attended the program got awards. The external stress—caused by the situation around you—is that you did not get the award. However, in this situation, you might experience internal stress, too: you might be disappointed in yourself for not pushing yourself to get up early and attend the program.

If you find that you are acting or feeling different than you normally do, ask yourself: "Am I stressed? Did something just happen that caused me to be stressed?" If you can figure out what kinds of situations cause you stress, then you will be better prepared to identify similar stress in the future.

❸ What Are Your Stress Triggers?

Some situations are likely to cause you stress each time they happen. These are known as your "stress triggers." That means that when those situations happen, you are likely to be uncomfortable. Figuring out your stress triggers can allow you to plan ahead and use strategies that can help you deal with the stress.

For example, did you know that some people get anxious before leaving for a vacation? They might love going on vacation, but at the same time, worry about whether they packed everything or whether they are going to miss anything while they're away. Others may be overwhelmed when there is too much noise in the house and not be able to focus on homework or activities they usually enjoy.

So, what are your stress triggers? Can you think of any situations that usually cause you stress? Again, knowing them allows you to plan ways to deal with them. You may want to write down your major stress triggers, so that you can look back at them later and try to use some of the strategies you will learn to help you to bounce back from them.

❹ Does Your Stress Ruin Good Times?

Have you ever been in a situation where you were having fun, and then suddenly you weren't? Maybe stress ruined the good times for you.

BRIAN'S *story*

Brian was a very busy twelve-year-old who was always hanging out with his friends and was usually smiling. During baseball practice one day, though, his coach noticed that Brian looked angry, and was very quiet, which was unlike him.

Brian's coach asked Brian if anything was bothering him. Brian shrugged his shoulders and answered honestly, "I guess I'm just in a bad mood." Brian knew he was sad and angry, yet he wasn't sure why. He was happy that he got an A on his math test earlier that day, and he was doing well at baseball practice.

That evening, Brian got into a fight with his older brother, Aaron, because Brian thought Aaron took his iPad without asking. Normally, this would not have bothered Brian. On this night, however, he screamed at Aaron and started crying. Then, suddenly, Brian finally understood why he had been upset all day. As he later told his dad, "I realized that the real reason I was in such a bad mood was because Aaron got into college and is going to leave home in August. I have all these weird thoughts and feelings about it. I am kind of angry that he is leaving, sad that he won't be in the house that much, and happy for him that he got into the school he wanted."

Once Brian figured out why he was upset, he could start trying to deal with the situation.

Have you ever had a day when you felt very emotional or found that a lot of situations bothered you more than they do on other days?

If you were Brian, what strategies would you use to deal with the stress?

Imagine you are eating lunch with friends and planning the song you are all going to sing and the costumes you are going to wear for the upcoming talent show. You love singing and had been really excited about the talent show. But you have a big social studies test right after lunch and are worried that you might fail it, your parents might be disappointed in your grade, and you might not even keep up the grade point average that you need to be on your sports team. You are under a lot of pressure. Who could concentrate, right?

Actually, there are ways to prepare so you aren't so stressed right before the big test. Let's say, though, that you just noticed that you are stressed during lunch before the test. Could you have fun at lunch anyway? If you think that you studied enough, can you calm yourself down, relax with your friends, and keep your stress from overwhelming you?

One great reason to work on becoming resilient is so that you can enjoy more of the fun times in your life. When a person is not resilient, and gets "stuck" being overwhelmed or stressed, it's harder to have fun. You may find that you are stuck for a minute or a day. Sometimes people get stuck for much longer, though. There are definitely some obstacles that will be hard to bounce back from right away. Resilience, though, helps people to bounce back slowly over time, and eventually enjoy themselves again, even though some tough times are never forgotten.

❺ Can You Name Your Emotion?

Finding the right word to identify the emotion you are experiencing can be a great way to understand yourself, share your emotions and thoughts with others, help others to understand you, and guess what? Deal with stress!

One way to do this is to think of your emotions on a scale of 1–10, with 10 being the strongest. If you are angry, is your reaction a 3? If so, maybe the word "annoyed" is right for you. Or is your reaction a 9? In that case, maybe the word "furious" is more appropriate.

For example, how might you feel, or what would you think, if a friend spread a rumor about you that wasn't true? If you told your friend that you were "a little uncomfortable when you spread that rumor in class yesterday," your friend might think it annoyed you but wasn't such a big deal.

Now, imagine if you told your friend that you were "furious and super embarrassed" about the same situation. Your friend might react differently, right? Finding accurate words for your emotions can even help you understand yourself better!

❻ How Do Other Kids Handle the Situation?

Pay special attention to how other kids handle stressful situations. Do other kids handle certain experiences or problems more easily than you do right now? You don't have to be upset if they are more resilient than you are in certain areas. In fact, you may actually be more resilient than they are in other areas!

If other people have found a way to bounce back from the situation that causes you stress, the good news is that you can learn from them about ways to cope! Watch and learn! In a situation that you find stressful, how do others handle it?

Pick out the kids who seem to be resilient and not overwhelmed by the situation that causes you stress. What are they doing? How are they handling the experience? Can you learn any coping strategies from them that you could use to reduce your own tension?

❼ What Strategies Can You Use?

Take a minute to ask yourself what strategies, or tools, you are already comfortable using to deal with your stress. Maybe it's time to add more tools for coping with tough times to your toolbox.

In later chapters you will read about some great strategies for dealing with stress and becoming more resilient, including positive self-talk, ways to relax and stay calm, and asking for advice and guidance.

But before finishing this chapter, know that patience is important as you develop resiliency skills. Becoming a resilient person doesn't happen overnight. If you now know what stresses you out, how you show that you are stressed, and how you feel when you are stressed, you are on your way to dealing with the stress. Patience lets you focus on learning resiliency skills.

Key Points

- Figuring out why you are stressed can help you to understand yourself better and then learn ways to cope.

- Knowing your stress triggers is an important step toward dealing with them.

- Getting "unstuck" or dealing with stressful times can allow you to have more fun times!

Conclusion

It's important to know yourself—what makes you happy and relaxed as well as what makes you stressed or uncomfortable. This chapter gave you some questions to ask yourself to figure out more about what makes you tick.

Are you ready to do a little more detective work? Did you know that even uncomfortable emotions like anger and sadness have a plus side? They can teach us about ourselves! Read on to find out more about what you can learn from your emotions and feelings.

CHAPTER THREE

Understanding Emotions

Anger, happiness, joy, sadness, guilt, and anxiety are emotions that almost everyone experiences at some time in their lives. The good thing about emotions, even the uncomfortable or unwanted ones, is that they can provide useful information. Emotions are clues to how you experience and think about things. Emotions can affect how your body feels or reacts. Like when you are happy, your body feels light and smiley. Or when you are angry, you might feel hot and tense. In this chapter, you will read about what you can learn from your emotions and feelings, what to do if you are an over-reactor or an under-reactor, and when you might want to share your emotions with others and get support.

Before reading the rest of this chapter, take a moment to take the quiz below about how well you understand your emotions:

When I am upset or angry at someone or something, I usually

a) feel guilty because it's wrong to be angry

b) realize that I'm angry but don't know what to do about it

c) know that I'm angry and have strategies to help me deal with it

When I have upsetting, sad, or angry feelings, I usually

a) try to ignore them and hope they will go away

b) let it all out and yell or cry

c) try to figure out why I have these feelings and how to deal with them

When feelings of happiness, anger, sadness, or disappointment are strong, I usually

a) don't know why but don't focus on it

b) recognize the emotion, but don't know what to do if I begin to feel uncomfortable

c) learn from my emotions and use them to help me to better understand myself

When I'm under stress, I usually

a) try not to focus on it and hide my stress from others

b) react strongly, by arguing with others or getting super anxious, for example

c) recognize when I'm stressed, know when I can deal with it, and when to ask for help

When I think about the purpose of emotions, I

a) think that emotions and feelings are annoying and wish I could just think and not be so emotional

b) enjoy having some emotions, such as happiness, but don't want to feel some others, such as sadness

c) know that all emotions remind me of how I'm reacting to myself, others, or to a situation, and they help me figure out how to cope

If you answered mostly "a": You may not like to focus on your emotions and you may try to ignore them. Understanding more about your emotions and feelings will help you figure out strategies to deal with them and bounce back when life seems to be stressful!

If you answered mostly "b": You can often identify your emotions but aren't always sure what strategies to use to handle tough times.

If you answered mostly "c": You can often identify your feelings and are able to learn from them. But keep reading this chapter to learn more about what your feelings may be telling you.

Emotions. Everyone Has Them, but Why?

Emotions give us the chance to love, to have pride, and to enjoy experiences. Without emotions, humans would be more like robots! Emotions teach us about what situations make us feel good, what makes us feel bad, what we like, and what we don't like.

Imagine if you never experienced anger, sadness, or anxiety. Sounds pretty good, right? But if you never had these emotions, it's likely that you wouldn't know when you were stressed (or in danger). Uncomfortable emotions like worry or anger are useful, because they can alert you when you are stressed or upset. Once you figure that out, you can work to change the situation—or how you think of the situation—for the better.

What Can You Learn From Your Emotions?

Emotions are important because they teach us about ourselves. When you recognize how you are feeling, you can figure out if there is anything you can do to change the situation or what you can do if you face a similar situation in the future. For example, Adam remembers getting an F on a book report in fourth grade because he didn't read the book, and guessed what the story was about based on the picture on the cover. Now he admits, "I hated getting that F. I was so mad at myself. I was also worried that I had disappointed my parents and my teacher. I never want to get that grade again. Sometimes, when I don't want to study or do my homework, I remember how bad I felt, and it reminds me to keep working hard."

Have you ever learned a lesson from a feeling? Having upsetting emotions can really teach you to avoid them! As long as you pay attention to what your feelings are telling you, you can work on how to handle situations in the future and can minimize the times you might become upset with yourself.

What can your emotions teach you? Once you have identified what you are feeling, try to answer the following questions:

- Am I comfortable with this?

- If I am comfortable, how can I work to keep feeling this way?

- If I am uncomfortable, is there anything I can do to change the situation that led me to have these emotions?

If you really pay attention to your emotions and feelings, you can decide whether to continue behaviors, change behaviors, seek help, or use coping strategies to get through a stressful situation, such as a test in class. Even when you can't change the situation, you can change how you react to it and deal with it.

People have a lot of control over their own actions. There will always be some situations you have no control over, though. What if you learn that your best friend's art project came in first place in a competition that you entered but didn't win? You most likely don't have the power to change the situation. You could be angry at your friend because you believe that you should have won, you could cry a lot, or even disown your friend because you are so jealous and angry. But none of these actions would take away your disappointment, right? Such actions might make you feel even worse! Instead, try to do things that make you feel better, such as:

- Share your disappointment with your parents or other trusted adults.

- Remember that not winning the competition does not make you a loser.

- Congratulate yourself for your willingness to enter the competition.

- Congratulate your friend.

- Ask for art tips from your friend or the art teacher.

- Take pride in your skills and the effort you put into the art project.

Any of these actions can help you to cope with not winning the art show. Plus, you would be being resilient!

MARISSA'S *story*

Marissa wanted to join the popular girls' group. Marissa began dressing like the kids in this group and let one of the popular kids cheat off of her on a test. Marissa didn't stop there. She also joined these popular kids on Instagram as they made fun of a new kid in class. Marissa was slowly being accepted by this group.

One night, though, Marissa had trouble falling asleep. She told her mother, "I am so sad, but I don't get it. I have this new group of great friends so I should be happy." Eventually, Marissa realized that her sadness was coming from the fact that she found her new behaviors—teasing a kid, dressing in a way that she really wasn't comfortable with, and letting a kid cheat off of her test paper—upsetting. When she changed her behavior, she started to be happier.

How did Marissa's emotions help her to understand her situation?

Has something like this ever happened to you?

If so, how did you handle your emotions and the situation?

What Kind of Rock Is It?

Do you know if your stress is caused by a situation that is serious, or by something that feels major but is really minor? When trying to figure out how large a problem or obstacle it is that you are facing, it's sometimes helpful to think in terms of pebbles, small rocks, large rocks, and boulders.

Picture yourself hiking up a mountain with friends. You are having fun and joking around. All of a sudden, you come across a pebble. What do you do? Do you stop the conversation and get stressed about how you can continue on the path even though there is a pebble on the ground? Probably not! A pebble is so small that you usually wouldn't even pay attention to it. Similarly, there are times in your life when you deal with situations without ever getting stressed. These are the pebble times.

Now, imagine that you are continuing on the hiking path with your friends and you come across a small rock. You may think, "Big deal!" and keep walking. You may kick it off to the side of the trail. Or you might think, "Oh no. If there are small rocks now, what if they get even bigger and I have to climb over them?" This thinking is called *anticipatory anxiety*—a worry about what *might* happen. Sometimes you might be worried about something that might happen, but when you stop and think about it, the problem you are currently facing is really a small one. You can use strategies described later in this book to help you to deal with bigger challenges…if they arise.

If you are hiking and come across a large rock, maybe two feet in diameter—a little larger than you could hug and connect your fingers around—this might be an obstacle. It is probably something you will notice. Some people might just walk on the part of the trail that is not covered by this large rock. Other people may want to walk on the side of the trail that is covered by this heavy and large rock and try to climb over it or push it aside. Similarly, sometimes problems are like large rocks: an obstacle, but one that you can deal with by using problem-solving strategies.

What if there is a boulder that blocks the entire path? You and your friends would all view this as an obstacle! You may need to brainstorm ways to go around the boulder, go over the boulder, or find another path to reach your destination (or goal). Brainstorming ways to handle obstacles is a useful tool and a resiliency skill!

Now, try to figure out if the stressful situation you are facing is a pebble, a small rock, a large rock, or even a boulder. Sometimes, kids think the situation is a boulder until they think about it more and decide it's actually a very annoying large rock–sized problem. Remember this key question: "Is the situation a minor or major problem, or no problem at all?"

A minor problem—or small to large rock—might be a situation that you react to but isn't that big of a deal when you think about it, such as being assigned to a different team than your best friend when you are playing a game of volleyball in your physical education class one day. Once you learn to be resilient, you may have momentary annoyance or disappointment about this situation, but you will know that you can get past this quickly.

A major problem—or a boulder—is something that you may not be able to fix or that may have more long-term consequences, such as being bullied at school, a parent losing a job, or a family member struggling with a serious medical illness. Even resilient people often seek support from others when dealing with major obstacles like these. Serious situations may require more time to deal with, although strategies for coping with stress can even be helpful in these very challenging times. Once you know how serious the obstacle you are facing is, you can figure out which resiliency tools to use to help you deal with it.

Are You an Over-Reactor or an Under-Reactor?

Sometimes adults or other kids may think that another person is "over-reacting" in a particular situation. At other times, they may wonder why a person isn't reacting much at all. So, what's the right amount of emotion to have?

Some people react strongly because it helps them avoid doing something or because they get attention from others. Other people may just experience their emotions super intensely and sometimes be overwhelmed by them. Still other people may guard their emotions and not let on when they are upset.

Samantha was an under-reactor. She hid her emotions and feelings, so no one really knew how she was reacting to the divorce of her parents. Samantha thought that people would admire and respect her if she pretended that nothing ever bothered her. What do you think of this plan? Being resilient, and moving forward even when times are tough, does not mean that you need to act like things don't bother you.

So how do you know if you are reacting the right amount when facing stress? Here's a quick exercise:

❶ On a scale of 1–10, with 10 being the most stressful, rate how stressful the situation is. Something super serious, such as having a life-threatening illness, would be a 10. This would be a boulder-sized problem!

❷ On a scale of 1–10, with 10 being the most upset, rate how upset you are in the situation. Being distraught, unable to cope, or overwhelmed are all descriptions that would be high on this scale.

Now, see if the number you listed in Step 1 of this exercise is close to the number you listed in Step 2. If the numbers are close, then you believe that your emotions fit the situation well.

What can you do if the numbers in this exercise don't match up closely? If you rated your upset feelings more highly than the seriousness of the situation, you may be reacting too strongly for the situation.

If you are an over-reactor, you may think that you are suffering and believe that the situation or obstacle is too much for you to handle. If this describes you, it may help you to know that it describes lots of other people, too, and that developing resiliency skills can help you.

If you are an **over-reactor**, see if any of the following suggestions help:

- Remind yourself that the situation is not going to kill you (if it might, you should get help from an adult immediately!).
- Use self-talk (you will learn about this in Chapter Four).
- Use calming strategies (you will learn about these in Chapter Five).
- Watch other kids and see how they deal with stress.
- Ask an adult about how they have handled similar obstacles in their own past.

If you are an **under-reactor**, it's important to know that:

- It does not mean that you are weak if you admit to having uncomfortable emotions.
- Admitting, at least to yourself, when you are upset or uneasy can allow you to use skills so that you can bounce back and cope.
- Emotions can be powerful. If you don't talk about them or at least understand them, you won't be able to figure out how they affect you—in your behavior, your sleep pattern, and your school work.
- Resilience does not mean that you aren't ever uncomfortable, overwhelmed, sad, or angry. It means that you can recognize these emotions and find ways to deal with them.

Resilient people may sometimes be overwhelmed. Resilient people may sometimes try to hide or forget about uncomfortable emotions. But resilient people are self-aware and can eventually focus on their strong or overwhelming emotions and use strategies to cope with them! Many resilient people have learned that they can often rely upon themselves to deal with stress, but that it is also a sign of emotional strength to know when to ask for help from others.

DID YOU KNOW?

When two researchers reviewed studies on how boys and girls show emotions, they discovered that girls expressed positive emotions as well as "sadness, fear, sympathy, (and) shame" more than boys did. Young boys expressed more of their anger than girls, but this switched during the teenage years. Does this mean that boys tend to be under-reactors and girls tend to be over-reactors? Not at all! It just reminds us that it's best to talk and ask others how they are doing rather than guessing. One boy and one girl, two girls, or two boys may even have the exact same emotions, but show them differently.

Chaplin, T.M. & Aldao, A. (2013). Gender differences in emotion expression in childhood: A meta-analytic review. *Psychological Bulletin, 139*(4), 735–765.

When Is It Okay to Rely on Others?

If you are experiencing uncomfortable emotions, you might not know when to ask adults for help or when to handle things alone. Here are four general ways that you might handle difficult situations:

❶ Ask an adult to fix the situation or make it go away.

❷ Ask an adult for guidance on how you can handle the situation.

❸ Figure out how to handle the situation yourself because you are confident that you can deal with it on your own.

❹ Do nothing or tell no one, while hoping that situation just goes away!

Try this quick exercise: for each situation below, think about how you would handle it, and then choose a course of action from numbers 1–4 above.

- ☐ You are scared and embarrassed because you are being kicked, teased, and threatened every day by a bully at school, even though you tried to ask him to stop.

- ☐ You are overwhelmed and anxious because you have to study for a test, but you also have soccer practice on the same night.

- ☐ You are hurt and sad because your friend isn't hanging around you so much, since she started hanging with a new kid at school.

What did you answer? If you are being bullied, or whenever you might be in danger, use option 1: ask for help! Adults can give you advice, and sometimes the bullying stops, but there are other times when the adult will need to step in to keep you safe. If you have studying and soccer practice on the same night, could you ask an adult for general suggestions or advice? If you think you can work things out directly by yourself, give it a try!

In the last example, if your friend is hanging out with a new kid and you have been left out, could you try option 3 and talk to your friend about how you feel? Even if your friend doesn't give you the answers you want, you could take pride in knowing that you tried to figure out what was going on. Then, you can decide whether you need or want to ask an adult for advice.

Take a minute to try to figure out when to ask for help and when to handle things independently. Adults can fix your problems sometimes, but if you let an adult take care of your problems frequently, you may not learn how to handle stress on your own.

On the other hand, if you never get help from adults, you may not get the chance to learn from their experience and their supportive suggestions. When you are uncomfortable, remember to use the rating scale of 1–10 that you read about earlier

CAROLINE'S *story*

Caroline knew that if she cried at home about something that happened at school, her mom would immediately call the school to ask them to handle the situation. Caroline's mom called the principal once to complain that Caroline's teacher didn't explain the math lesson in a way that made any sense.

Caroline was glad that her mom wanted her to be happier and less stressed. But Caroline never had the chance to try to understand the math lesson on her own before her mom stepped in. So, the next month, when she didn't understand a science lesson, she didn't think to ask for help from her teacher or friends because she knew that her mother would take care of the situation by calling her teacher and getting the information that she needed. Caroline didn't realize that she could have handled the situation independently by talking with her teacher and getting clarification about the science lesson and homework.

What else could Caroline have done to help herself understand the science lesson, before talking to her mom?

Have you ever relied on your parent when you could have handled the situation on your own? If so, how did that work out?

in this chapter. If you are at an 8, 9, or 10, that means that you are super stressed, emotionally very uncomfortable, and it's time to talk with an adult. You may decide to ask an adult for suggestions and then handle things on your own, or it may be important for the adult to step in and support you by taking action.

Key Points

- Emotions help us learn more about ourselves!

- It's okay to rely on others as long as you also rely on yourself.

- Learning to accept your emotions is an important step toward becoming resilient!

Summary

This chapter explored the fact that emotions can be a guide to understanding yourself and how you are handling or reacting to a situation. Some people may find that they are under-reactors or over-reactors. There are times when even the most resilient individuals benefit from asking others for help. However, there are also some situations you can try to handle independently.

Some emotions can be uncomfortable to experience. So what can you do about them? In the next chapter you will learn about one great strategy for dealing with uncomfortable emotions: self-talk.

CHAPTER FOUR

Using Self-Talk

Resilient people use many strategies and tools for dealing with obstacles and difficult times. You can learn how to use these tools too! One of the most powerful tools is something called "self-talk."

First, take a minute to see how much you already know about self-talk:

When someone tells me to use self-talk or to talk to myself, I

a) don't know what they are talking about

b) recognize that self-talk helps some people feel better, but I don't know how to do that

c) understand that self-talk helps and want to figure out more ways to use it to be resilient

When I want to build up my confidence, I

a) am not sure what to say to myself

b) stop calling myself names, like "stupid"

c) say nice things to myself, like I would say if I were talking to a friend

When I make a mistake while trying a new activity, I

a) give up and avoid doing that activity ever again

b) am embarrassed but try to get over it

c) remind myself that mistakes are part of learning and keep trying

When I want to reach a goal, I

a) talk myself out of it using words like "I can't" or "I won't"

b) just keep hoping that everything will work out

c) encourage myself to work hard and practice so I can reach my goal

I use self-talk to practice what I might say when I'm in a stressful situation

a) never

b) sometimes

c) often

If you answered mostly "a": It sounds like you do not yet use self-talk. Read on to find out more about the value of self-talk and how it can help you to become more resilient.

If you answered mostly "b": You have already started using the tool of self-talk. Keep reading to learn even more about how it can help.

If you answered mostly "c": Congratulations! You are well on your way to mastering this strategy for helping you to become resilient. You may find some more ideas for how to use self-talk in this chapter.

Self-Talk

There are two very different kinds of self-talk: helpful and unhelpful. Helpful self-talk allows you to gain courage, resilience, and comfort. Unhelpful self-talk can make you more upset and more overwhelmed.

Helpful self-talk is similar to what you might say to friends to help them to feel better. For example, if your friend was upset because she came in fifth in a bicycle race, you might say something like, "You had a rough day. You know you usually bike faster. Maybe you were just tired. Maybe talk to your coach and you can figure out what happened." Would this help your friend? Probably. You didn't blame the other racers, you complimented your friend on her general skill level, and you gave her a suggestion—speaking to her coach—that might help.

Now, imagine if you said, "You really stunk today. I think you found out that you can't really compete with these good bikers. Give it up!" Your friend would probably get upset with you and feel even more defeated. This is unhelpful talk. Many people use this kind of self-talk, and even call themselves harsh names such as "loser" or "idiot." Unhelpful self-talk can bring you down instead of helping you to gain the confidence to overcome challenges.

Luckily, helpful self-talk can get rid of the unhelpful self-talk if you let it. It's like these two kinds of talk battle inside of you. Donny was upset, on his first day ever playing tennis, when he couldn't hit the tennis ball so that it went over the net and back to the other player. He felt like a loser until he used helpful self-talk. Check out his thoughts (his internal dialogue) below:

His **unhelpful** self-talk: "I'm such a loser. I kept missing the ball or hitting it into the net and not over it. I'm never going to play again."

His **helpful** self-talk: "Big deal. You missed the ball a lot. It's your first time playing tennis. Congratulate yourself. You were brave to try it."

His **unhelpful** self-talk: "I bet other kids think I'm a loser, too. They all probably play better than me, even on their first day learning."

His **helpful** self-talk: "Most kids focus more on themselves than on others, so some kids probably didn't even notice that you missed the ball. Also, if you laugh *with* yourself, let others know it's your first time playing, and you want help from them, most kids will not laugh at you."

His **unhelpful** self-talk: "But what if someone does laugh at me?"

His **helpful** self-talk: "Do you really want to feel bad about yourself or not go back to tennis just because some kid laughs?"

His **unhelpful** self-talker finally says: "Okay. Good point!"

See how helpful self-talk is like being a supportive friend to yourself? Give it a try. It may feel a little uncomfortable to do this at first, until you get the hang of it. Once you get the hang of it, though, it can be a very powerful tool to help you to feel better about yourself, your mistakes, and your ability to deal with stress.

Here are some examples of encouraging thoughts you can tell yourself when you are using helpful self-talk:

- Most mistakes don't change the course of your entire life.
- Mistakes can be learning opportunities.
- No one is perfect. Even Olympic champions aren't perfect every day and in every area of their lives!
- Having the courage to deal with an obstacle or challenge puts you on the path toward resilience.
- Stress can feel uncomfortable, but there are ways to deal with it, either on your own, or with the guidance and support of others.

When you talk to yourself, using "I can" or "I can try" or "I will" or "I will try" helps a lot, while saying "I can't" or "I won't try" is counter-productive. Keep your self-talk realistic. Sometimes what you say to yourself can make you feel good, but may not be true or even realistic. For example, you could tell yourself, "I should be an NBA player. It doesn't matter that I don't practice my free throws. I'm sure I'll be a star on an NBA team!" In reality, not practicing would not be helpful no matter what you tell yourself! Instead, work hard, focus on realistic goals, and use self-talk that motivates you.

Danger, Danger! Self-Talk Traps

Realistic, helpful self-talk can help you focus on your abilities and think of possible back-up plans or alternative strategies that you can try. You can also build resilience if you can brainstorm ways to move past a difficult situation. Self-talk can help you to remind yourself that you have survived other uncomfortable situations and can get through the current one as well.

LENA'S *story*

Lena wanted to excel in all her science and math classes so that she could get into medical school and become a doctor. When Lena found out that she didn't get into the honors class for biology, she told herself, "I'm a total failure. Some of my friends who don't even want to be doctors got into the honors class and I couldn't. I guess I'm not going to be a doctor. I guess I am not smart enough!"

Lena talked with her guidance counselor at school. The guidance counselor helped Lena change her attitude. Lena told herself, "I'm super disappointed that I didn't get into the honors class. I think I didn't take studying too seriously this year and that's why my science grades weren't good enough. I can get better grades if I work hard. I know that if I get high grades in school, I can still get into a great college. If I get into a great college, I can still think about going to medical school!"

Lena tried harder in school after figuring out how to use realistic, helpful self-talk.

How do you think the unhelpful self-talk made Lena feel? How do you think she felt after switching to helpful self-talk?

Have you ever felt like Lena?

If so, what did you do?

There are a few common "traps" to watch out for when you use self-talk that might get you stuck. Check out some of these examples and think about whether you use any of these ways of thinking to get yourself stuck or trapped.

All-or-Nothing Thinking

All-or-nothing thinking means thinking that everything is either great or awful—nothing is "okay" or "so-so." Sometimes a person who likes things to be just perfect can get stuck in this all-or-nothing thinking—either everything is perfect and wonderful or everything is awful.

Hannah fell into this trap. She was upset when she learned that she "only got a 96" on her math test. She focused on why she lost points and why she didn't answer all of the questions correctly. After learning how to use helpful self-talk, she started thinking a little differently. She explained, "I now try to focus on the fact that I got 96 out of 100 points on the test. That's pretty good! I also spoke to my teacher about my errors and now I understand why I came up with the two wrong answers. I'm proud of the fact that I did well on the test and that I learned why I lost points." Hannah ended up feeling good about her test grade and her follow-through on learning from her mistakes!

Letting Mistakes Ruin Experiences

Everyone makes mistakes. You may make a mistake when you are learning something new or even during everyday life. Do you remember your mistakes? Some people make mistakes and then totally avoid doing that activity ever again so they won't make that same mistake in the future. These people don't know how to bounce back. Resilient people know strategies to help them to deal with mistakes so that they don't ruin an experience.

Max went to an ice-skating party, even though he had never gone ice skating before. He needed help just lacing up his skates. Once on the ice, he took a step and immediately fell. However, instead of getting embarrassed or letting the mistake ruin his time at the party, he laughed and said, "I guess I should have worn bumpers on my butt!" His friends laughed with him, not at him. They helped him up and gave him tips for getting his balance. Max had a great time at the party!

When you are faced with situations that are a challenge, can you think of them as adventures? Can you laugh about mistakes? Can you just enjoy the adventure or experience?

Treating Friends Better Than You Treat Yourself

Many people don't realize it, but they actually treat friends better than they treat themselves. Lots of kids would be supportive of their friends, if their friends were disappointed with a grade or struggled during a competition. They might encourage them to ask for help, review their answers, continue to practice and learn, but also to remember that a low grade or struggling in a skill does not mean they are dumb or stupid. But sometimes, kids engage in name-calling toward themselves. They forget to be nice to themselves. Sophia made it to the spelling bee finals in her school. On the day of the finals, she was nervous because she and the other finalists were on stage with the rest of the students watching them. When it was Sophia's turn to spell a word, she made a mistake. She ended up being the first finalist out of the competition. Later that day, Sophia talked with a friend and said, "I can't believe I couldn't spell that word. It wasn't even that hard. I'm such an idiot. I was the first one out. I'm never going to be in a spelling bee again! I'm so embarrassed!"

Sophia was in a bad mood for the rest of the afternoon. Later that evening, her older sister told her not to be so hard on herself and that she'd never treat a friend that way. Eventually, Sophia's thoughts about the spelling bee changed. She said, "The truth is that I made it to the finals. This was my first time! I should be proud of that. I am a good speller! Next time, I may just take more time to think before rushing to spell the words. I don't have to win. I just have to try my best."

Do you fall into the same trap of treating friends better than you treat yourself? Next time you are disappointed with your actions or your ability to deal with stress, try imagining what you would say to a friend to help him or her calm down and feel better. Then, say it to yourself. It's a great way to get out of this trap!

Exaggerating Feelings

Have you ever used dramatic language or viewed a small rock as a boulder and felt totally overwhelmed? Here is an example: "I'm mortified that everyone saw me drop my food in the cafeteria. I can never go back there. All the other kids must think I'm so uncoordinated. My social life is ruined. I'm a total klutz. I'm so depressed." Was it really such a significant event? Making this situation bigger than it was is exaggerating the situation and intensifying this student's feelings.

Let's try turning Anna's unhelpful thoughts into helpful self-talk. Anna told her mother, "If I don't get first chair in the clarinet, I'll just die." Really? Instead, she could think this: "I know that only one person can get first chair in the clarinet section of the band. I will practice the clarinet and work to improve my playing. I still want to be first chair, but I'll be happy just knowing I'm improving!"

Now take a moment to think about whether you ever exaggerate the seriousness of situations and intensify your own emotions. If so, try substituting the unhelpful thoughts with helpful ones. It may help you to cope with the situation once you realize that it may not be as extreme of a situation as you originally feared.

Believing That Waiting for Something Equals Emotional Torture

Have you ever waited in a long line and been frustrated or so bored that you felt that it was almost painful to stay there? Being patient and waiting can be great skills to learn. Rather than thinking that waiting is equal to torture because it annoys you, try using helpful self-talk.

Here is a helpful self-talk response that worked for Colin: "Waiting isn't fun, but I can think about something good, like my birthday party, and plan what the party will be like and who will be there! It can make the waiting better. I now find that waiting sometimes gives me time to think!"

Believing That You Always Have to Be Number One and Get Applause

Many people love winning a competition, being stronger or better than others in a particular skill, and getting recognized by others as being special. Applause is nice, but do you need it? What if you try hard but aren't the best in a particular subject, sport, or other activity?

Lizzy loved when people complimented her and applauded when she finished acting in one of the school plays. She loved when she finished first in her school's one-mile race. However, this year, Lizzy placed fourth in the race. She didn't get a trophy. Only her family and best friend congratulated her.

At first, Lizzy used unhelpful self-talk. She said, "No one really applauded. I have no trophy. I didn't finish first. I guess I was a better runner last year. I think I'm quitting running. It's not fun when I don't win."

Lizzy talked with her parents, running coach, and with her best friend about how discouraged she felt about running and the race. Her coach taught her how to use helpful self-talk. Eventually, Lizzy learned to accept the fact that she was a good runner, she liked to run, and she didn't always need to win: "No one is always number one. If I always try to be the best me, then I can look in the mirror and feel proud of myself without needing tons of applause from others!"

If you expect yourself to be perfect and always need to win and get applause, that can cause a lot of stress! It's also unrealistic. That's really not bad news. It's good news! Giving yourself realistic expectations can reduce some of the pressure that you might feel if you believe that you always have to be number one and get tons of recognition from others.

DID YOU KNOW?

Have you ever heard of the term "emotional intelligence"? There are a bunch of different definitions of this, but basically people are thought to have emotional intelligence if they can regulate their emotions, strive to reach goals, and problem-solve to find healthy and productive ways to handle situations that they may encounter. Does this describe you? Did you know that researchers found that self-talk can help you to have more emotional intelligence? So, why not give it a try?

Depape, A.R., Hakin-Larson, J., Voelker, S., Page, S., & Jackson, D.L. (2006). Self-talk and emotional intelligence in university students. *Canadian Journal of Behavioural Science, 38*(3), 250–260.

Role-Playing With Self-Talk

Another way that self-talk can be helpful is that it can help us to role-play how we can handle a situation before we actually are in that situation. That's right—you can role-play conversations, even if you are all alone!

Sometimes you may want to—or need to—have an uncomfortable conversation with another person. Perhaps you feel left out by a friend, or you have to tell your parents that you decided to learn how to play the clarinet when they wanted you to learn the saxophone. Whether you are trying to have a conversation that might get emotional or you are just trying to express yourself clearly, practicing speaking your part of the conversation to yourself can help.

Try looking in the mirror at home and telling yourself what you want to tell another person. Remember:

- Be respectful.
- Be clear in how you feel, but don't assume you know how the other person feels.
- Avoid accusing the other person or threatening him or her.
- Include a suggestion on how you can both move forward, or bounce back, from this time in your lives.

Practicing the conversation with yourself helps you know what you want to say to the other person, and be comfortable and confident in how you will say it. This can help you to deal with the stress, overcome obstacles, and become more resilient!

Key Points

- Helpful self-talk moves you toward resilience—unhelpful self-talk can get you stuck!
- Helpful self-talk can help you to feel better!
- You can use self-talk to help you role-play difficult conversations.

Summary

In this chapter, you read about the benefits of using helpful self-talk: it helps you be supportive of yourself. You also learned about how some kinds of self-talk can keep you from being resilient. Lastly, you read about how self-talk can help you to role-play conversations that you might want to—or need to—have with others.

Using self-talk is only one building block toward resilience. In the next few chapters, you will learn even more ways to get "unstuck" when life gets tough.

CHAPTER FIVE

Calming Yourself

Have you ever tried to take a test or concentrate on learning something new, but you were super nervous, sad, or mad? Your emotions can get in the way, right? It can be pretty tough to deal with the challenges of taking a test or learning new material on top of being extremely emotional and stressed out. But you'll find it easier to problem-solve, cope, and face challenges if you are calm first! In this chapter, you will read about ways to calm yourself and get a handle on your emotions. Calming strategies are an important part of being resilient, and will help you get things done!

First, take a moment to think about how you calm down and what strategies you may already use:

When I'm super stressed or emotional, I

a) am usually not even aware of it

b) know that I'm super stressed or emotional, but I'm not sure what to do about it

c) realize that I'm having strong emotions but know what to do to become more relaxed and calm

Once I'm calm, I

a) still have a lot of difficulty finding solutions to my problems

b) can talk to my parents about how to handle some tough situations

c) have a variety of strategies for handling challenges in my life

When it comes to breathing, I

a) have no idea how to use my breathing to help me calm down

b) know it's important not to hold my breath when I'm stressed

c) know breathing techniques that can help me to calm down

When I want to calm myself, I

a) just try not to think about the stress in my life

b) have one strategy—I talk to my parents and they help me

c) do lots of different things and use different strategies at different times to calm down

If someone told me to use my imagination, memories, and thoughts to calm down, I would

a) have no idea how to do this

b) try it, but I wouldn't really know how to do it

c) talk to myself (use self-talk), focus on pleasant memories, and use my imagination to picture a how I want things to turn out

If you answered mostly "a": You may be struggling to find ways to calm down and problem-solve. Read on to learn about strategies you might find useful.

If you answered mostly "b": You already have some ways to deal with stress, but it's always helpful to have many tools to help you when you want to calm down.

If you answered mostly "c": You use a lot of calming strategies and are well on your way to being resilient. Continue reading, you might learn more!

Calming Strategies

Simply put, when you are calm, you will likely find that it is easier to figure out what is causing your stress and ways to deal with it. There are many different ways for people to calm down. Some kids calm down after playing a sport and burning off a lot of energy, other kids might sit quietly and focus on relaxing thoughts, while still others may calm down best by talking with a parent or friend. You have to experiment a bit to find out what works for you.

As you read about the different types of calming strategies, try each one out and make a note of the ones that work best for you. This way, when you are upset, you already know which techniques you want to try.

Remember that once you are calm, you can more easily brainstorm ways to cope with the situation! Here are some specific tips that might help you to calm down:

Breathing Exercises

Did you know that the way you breathe can either increase your feelings of being upset or calm you down? It's true!

Most people change their breathing without even thinking about it. Imagine if someone jumped out of a closet when you went to open it. You may take in a large gulp of air because you are surprised. You don't think about doing this. You just do it.

When you are happy and calm, you breathe at a certain regular pace. In and out, in and out. Your body takes control of how much oxygen you need and when to let the carbon dioxide out. When you are nervous, your body reacts to prepare you to deal with danger, whether by fighting, running away, or freezing. The technical name for this is the "fight, flight, or freeze" response. This response can cause you to breathe super fast, or even to forget to breathe.

You can teach yourself how to breathe in a relaxed way, which relaxes your body so you are better able to deal with life's stresses. When you are feeling stressed, try this exercise:

❶ Slowly fill up your lungs with air by breathing in slowly through your nose. It might help to pretend that you are slowly taking in the smell of freshly-baked cookies, or your favorite meal—don't rush the breathing.

❷ Hold the breath and slowly count to three.

❸ Slowly let the air out, through your mouth. It might help to blow out the air by imagining that you are trying to gently move a feather along your desk.

Repeat steps 1–3 several times until you can continue breathing calmly while focusing on other strategies to deal with the stress and bounce back. Of course, in the unlikely event that you feel lightheaded, then skip this strategy—there are tons of others to use.

JACK'S *story*

Jack always became anxious when he had to give an oral presentation in class. He told his teacher, "I feel like I run out of oxygen. I try to say everything quickly and with only one breath. I know how to talk and breathe. I do it all the rest of my life, except not when I'm in front of the class." Jack's teacher helped Jack to review his presentation and practice how much to say before pausing (and breathing).

Jack drew large, orange periods on his note cards to remind him that the sentence was over and he needed to breathe. Guess what? It worked! Afterwards, Jack said, "That was the first presentation where I didn't feel like I would die from not breathing enough. I breathed after every sentence." Jack now knows that he can deal with these kinds of stressful times, be more resilient, and have oxygen to spare!

Tricia, on the other hand, breathed too fast when she was very upset or nervous. She explained, "When my Spanish teacher told us we were getting a pop quiz, I started panicking. I thought I would fail. I started breathing really fast and thinking, "Oh no, oh no, what am I going to do?" Breathing too fast increased her physical tension, her feelings of anxiety, and her feeling that she was unable to cope with this stress.

What do you think of Jack's idea to draw reminders on his notecards?

What could Tricia do to calm herself when she starts breathing too fast?

Have you ever felt like Jack or Tricia?

Physical Exercise

Some people know that they deal with obstacles and tough times better after they exercise. There are chemicals inside the human brain that help people to feel better. Endorphins, for example, are very useful for helping us to deal with pain or stress. Have you ever gone for a run "to clear your head" and felt better afterwards? Those are your endorphins at work!

Not everyone likes running. If you don't enjoy running, think about how you feel after you play a sport, run around a lot doing chores, or even after you do other kinds of physical activity, such as yoga or tai chi. If you know that your body feels more relaxed and your heart rate calms down after a workout or other physical activity, then this strategy may help you to battle stress.

Take a minute to think about how you breathe when you are stressed and how you react to stress after you exercise. Knowing how your body works and what you can do to help it to relax are both important as you work to calm down.

DID YOU KNOW?

Did you know that there is a part of your brain that helps you to feel calm? A part of the brain called the prefrontal cortex helps us to adjust our emotions so that they aren't always super powerful and overwhelming. This is important so that we can calm down and not be overwhelmed by emotions such as anxiety. Research suggests that if we are calmer, it might be easier for us to pay attention and learn!

Since you are most likely learning inside and outside of school, knowing the tools to calm down may allow you to more easily take in new experiences and new learning! Knowing how to use calming skills is important to use now and in the future. Now you know that there is a specific part of your brain to help you to calm down!

Lantieri, L. (2008). The resilient brain: Building inner resilience. *Reclaiming Children and Youth, 17*(2), 43–46.

Calming Imagery

Calming imagery is a fun strategy to practice. It's all about using your senses—vision, hearing, smell, touch, taste—to relax or reduce that feeling of being emotionally overwhelmed. This strategy works partly because it lets your brain focus on something other than the upsetting situation, but also because thinking of calming times can lead to calming emotions.

Okay, let's begin. Here are some examples of how you can use your senses to think about stress-free times:

❶ **Vision:** Imagine seeing "You Beat the Game!!!" on your videogame screen, or seeing your pet jumping up and down with joy when you walk in the door of your home.

❷ **Hearing:** Imagine hearing your dad compliment you for something you did recently, or imagine the pleasant sound of birds chirping outside of your window.

❸ **Smell:** Imagine the smell of your favorite food, or a smell that reminds you of a good memory, like the smell of mud after you and a bunch of your friends slipped while playing football and laughed and laughed about the experience.

❹ **Touch:** Imagine being hugged by your mom, or cuddling with your favorite pet, or even the touch of your blanket over you as you feel safe and comfortable in your bed.

❺ **Taste:** Imagine the taste of your favorite meal or dessert or imagine the taste of the salt air as you walk along the sand near the ocean.

Each of the images above can calm some people. Try to imagine your favorite time on vacation. Can you picture it, hear the sounds, and recall some of the smells, tastes, and even things you touched? The more images you can remember, and the more senses you can engage, the more realistic the memory can be.

Now it's your turn. What memories or experiences make you feel good? Maybe you have a favorite vacation spot, or maybe you like to be curled up in bed with a good book. You could even use your imagination to make up a movie that uses your senses and takes you to a wonderful place in your mind that relaxes you. For example, Michael told his aunt, "I always picture myself finding a planet, being the king, and then flying up all the people I love and starting towns and cities."

CARLY'S *story*

Using your senses to calm down can even be useful when you are experiencing boulder-sized obstacles. When Carly's parents got divorced, her dad moved 2,000 miles away. Carly loved her dad and missed him terribly. During one of their frequent phone conversations, her dad said, "Carly, when we aren't talking on the phone and aren't visiting, I'm still with you. Picture the good times we always have when we are together. Then, the next time we talk, tell me about the experience you thought of."

Carly tried her dad's suggestion. The next time she was sad that she was separated from her father, she recalled the time they went to a carnival and her dad kept winning stuffed animals for her. She remembered how the carnival and her dad looked, the sounds of activity around her, the smell of the food being served throughout the carnival, the warm touch of her dad's arm around her and the stuffed animals in her arms, and the taste of cotton candy that she had just before they left the carnival.

She later told her father, "It works pretty good. I used to cry every night when I was trying to fall asleep because I miss you. I couldn't deal with the divorce and stuff. Now, I still sometimes cry, but thinking of our fun times and knowing we'll talk about which one I picked is kind of a fun thing."

Carly used her senses, and memories, to calm herself down. Even though she couldn't change the fact that her parents were divorced, she was now able to relax and enjoy her daily activities: friends, music, and times with her mom.

What do you think of Carly's dad's suggestion?

Have you ever faced a boulder-sized obstacle? Do you think you could use your senses and your memories to help yourself feel better too?

There is no limit to your imagination! Take out a sheet of paper, and try to list a few memories or scenarios that make you laugh or smile. Then, when really upset or overwhelmed, you can remember them.

Calming Thoughts

Remember reading about self-talk in Chapter Four? One calming technique is to combine calming imagery with calming and helpful words—this is a special kind of self-talk. When life seems difficult, you can try the following thoughts (along with using your senses to focus on positive and calming imagery):

- Remember other times when you got through stress.

- Remind yourself that you can ask others for help.

- Remind yourself that you have tools now to calm yourself. Remember that it's okay to sometimes feel emotional pain and that it's just a reminder that you need to find a way to cope with the stress.

- Remember that running away from a tough time doesn't teach you how to deal with it.

- Remember that dealing with a tough time helps you to be more resilient and have more confidence that you can handle future stressful situations.

- Remember that there are consequences to your actions, so think about the consequence you want and ways to get it.

Does this sound like a lot to remember? You may want to write down these tips and put the paper in a place that you can find it easily if you are stressed. Once you get in the habit of using calming thoughts, it should get easier to do!

Distraction

Did you know that sometimes simply distracting yourself can calm you enough to deal with stress? Brooke, for example, said, "Whenever I feel panicked about not understanding my homework, I cope better if I take a break, do something relaxing, then try again. I usually figure out the assignment once I'm calmer."

Try to de-focus—or stop focusing on the stress for a while—and see if it helps. Perhaps you can spend a short period of time drawing, singing, Skyping, listening to music, or shooting baskets outside. Once you are calm and refreshed, you might find that you can deal with the problem better!

Seeking out a Support Team

Remember that resilient people are comfortable handling some situations on their own, sometimes getting advice from others on how to deal with stress, and feel comfortable asking for others to help out when it's needed. It's not a sign of weakness to ask for help when you are facing a large or boulder-sized problem—in fact, it is a sign of strength to get help when help is needed!

Key Points

- When you are overwhelmed, calming yourself can increase your ability to think of ways to cope!

- There are many ways to calm yourself—find the ones that work best for you.

- Self-talk and using your senses and imagery can be fun tools to help you to calm down!

Summary

In this chapter, you read about the fact that being calmer allows you to think more clearly about how to deal with tough times and be more resilient. You learned some important strategies for calming yourself: breathing exercises, physical activity, calming imagery and thoughts, distraction, and seeking help. In the next chapter, you will get a chance to read about ways to bounce back from disappointments and common sources of stress.

CHAPTER SIX

Handling Decisions, Disappointments, and New Challenges

You have now read a lot about becoming a resilient person! Now, it's time to learn how resilient people use coping skills to get through stressful experiences. Learning ways to make decisions, deal with disappointments, and adjust to new situations gives you confidence and helps you bounce back! Before you read this chapter, take this quiz to see how you are using coping skills:

When I have to make a decision, I

a) put it off and hope someone else makes the decision for me

b) make decisions that I find easy, but ask other people to make the big decisions

c) make decisions and know how to think about decision making

When I am disappointed, I

a) often get really sad or really mad

b) try to stay calm

c) know how to use helpful self-talk to get through it

When I am calm, I

a) still have trouble bouncing back from disappointment

b) deal with disappointment a little better, but not great

c) can come up with some creative ways to overcome or deal with disappointment

When I'm under stress, I

a) look for quick ways to get rid of my stress

b) know that sometimes quick solutions to problems aren't always the right solutions, but I'm not sure how to work toward more long-term and better solutions

c) know how to come up with quick solutions, but also feel confident working on more long-term solutions

When I am in a new situation, I

a) usually feel uncomfortable and don't know what to do

b) stay close to my parents or my friends

c) usually view the experience as an adventure!

If you answered mostly "a": You could benefit from working on how to solve problems, handle disappointment, and deal with new experiences.

If you answered mostly "b": You have some strategies to deal with common sources of stress, but could learn more.

If you answered mostly "c": You are well on your way to being resilient! However, even you may learn some tips in this chapter!

Creative Decision Making

Did you know that making decisions can cause feelings of frustration, disappointment, anger, and anxiety? Sometimes kids—and even adults!—get overwhelmed when trying to make decisions. There are people who can't cope with decision making when they need to make choices. However, many people can find a solution if they think creatively rather than simply saying "yes" or "no" to different choices.

DID YOU KNOW?

Researchers have reported that it can be easier to get used to a new situation or problem-solve if, when faced with a dilemma or difficulty, you view the experience as an opportunity. So next time instead of thinking about challenges as obstacles, reframe them as opportunities. Try out new strategies for overcoming challenges. Give it a try—it may make coping with stress a little easier!

Marcketti, S.B., Karpova, E., & Barker, J. (2009). Creative problem-solving exercises and training in FCS. *Journal of Family and Consumer Sciences, 101*(4), 47–48.

An example may help you to understand how creative decision making works. Abigail really wanted to go with her friend Sydney and her parents to an amusement park on Saturday. Her mother thought that would be fun and agreed she could go. This would be the perfect day for Abigail to hang out with her friend.

But everything changed when Abigail and her mother realized that her music competition was also on Saturday morning. Abigail became really upset. She loved music and was excited about participating in the competition. Abigail started crying and became angry. She told her mother, "Fine! I'll give up my entire social life for some stupid competition. Or, maybe I'll just drop out of the competition. Who cares about music?"

Abigail found herself in a "cognitive circle without end." That means that her thoughts didn't lead to a solution. Instead, she kept switching between dropping her social life, dropping her music, dropping her social life, dropping her music, and on and on. She wasn't trying to find a way to cope with this situation, was she?

Abigail then used calming strategies and helpful self-talk to get ready to find a way to make a decision. She asked her mother to help, and they easily came up with a creative plan: Immediately after the competition, Abigail's mother would drive her to meet up with her friend. They would pack a lunch, so they could eat on the way and not waste time stopping for food. Abigail learned that sometimes creative planning can lead to having both activities that she wanted.

Have you ever been in a similar situation to Abigail? How did you handle it? Abigail figured out a compromise, by giving up part of the time doing one activity so she could still do both: go to the competition and hang out afterwards with her friend at the amusement park. This is definitely one way to bounce back from these kinds of time conflicts.

Dealing With Disappointment

Most people can remember a time when they were disappointed. Disappointment usually occurs when you expected or hoped for one outcome and it didn't work out the way you wanted. Some people may just say "oh well," while others may be sad or even angry. Have you ever been disappointed? Did you have ways to deal with it?

When Brent's science fair project didn't win, he was incredibly disappointed. After all, he had put a great deal of time into the project and thought he should win. He was angry at the winner for "taking *my* prize," he was angry at the judge for not recognizing his project as exceptional, and he spent the next few days being angry all the time. Has something like this ever happened to you?

Here are some tips for coping with disappointment:

- Remind yourself that it's okay to be annoyed or frustrated.
- Use calming strategies to relax so that you can think clearly.
- Use self-talk to remind yourself that this isn't a catastrophe and you can survive it.
- Make sure to avoid taking out your frustration on other people who aren't trying to purposely hurt or annoy you.
- If you have to miss out on a goal, plan a way to reach this goal in the future, if possible.

- Talk with others about your disappointment. They may be able to help you come up with a way to cope.

- Compliment yourself for handling the stress of disappointment!

Now you know that there are strategies for dealing with disappointment. Walking around being sad or angry doesn't change the situation. However, calming yourself, changing your self-talk, and complimenting yourself for handling the stress of disappointment can all help you to deal with these times more comfortably.

DID YOU KNOW?

Did you know that students who demonstrate leadership skills know that disappointments may happen, but still take on challenges anyway? These students know that it is common to sometimes experience disappointments or even failure.

If you share the same view as the student leaders, then you can try new experiences without worrying that you will be devastated by obstacles, disappointments, or failures. It can make life less stressful to think this way!

Rice, D. (2011). Qualities that exemplify student leadership. *Techniques, 86*(5), 28–31.

Quick Solutions vs. the Right Solutions

Coming up with solutions to conflicts or problems may take more time than a person wants to devote to thinking about them. This can be very frustrating and create disappointment. However, taking your time to think carefully about the situation and how your decision affects your goals (or what you want to accomplish in this situation) helps you actually reach your goals. So take your time! The quick solution might not always be the right solution! It's better to put in time now thinking about how to deal with an obstacle. Otherwise you might end up spending even more time later trying to deal with both the obstacle and an unfortunate and impulsive reaction.

Daniella, for example, was stressed over studying for a midterm exam. Her quick solution was not to focus on studying and to do things that relaxed her instead, such as drawing and playing videogames. However, the night before the test, she panicked as she realized that her quick solution only led to her procrastinating. Now, she was running out of time before the test, she still needed to study, she never came up with a study strategy, and she was mad at herself for procrastinating.

Taking on New Challenges

You will always face challenges. That's life! Some challenges are annoying or frustrating, like having to take a test in your least favorite subject, while other challenges can be exciting, such as learning to drive a car.

New experiences or challenges can be stressful. Do you remember learning to swim or ride a bike? Were you perfect at it right away? Probably not! Most people make mistakes when learning how to do something they have not done before. These errors or mistakes can be viewed as pebbles, rocks, or even boulders, depending on how you think about them.

If you think you should master a task instantly or be good at everything you do right away, you open yourself up to disappointment. The excitement of new experiences disappears if every mistake upsets you. Being upset about mistakes could lead you to avoid new learning experiences. Avoiding new experiences may keep you from being able to manage life's challenges and stresses. On the other hand, accepting that new experiences are learning opportunities, and that mistakes are key parts of that learning opportunity, can help you to bounce back from mistakes and become resilient!

Before reading the rest of this chapter, take a few minutes to think about new experiences you would like to have. What do you think about trying them? If you look at new experiences as fun and exciting times, then you probably already know that you can learn from the situation, bounce back from mistakes you might make, and be confident that you can enjoy the experience!

SUSAN'S *story*

Susan struggled to accept the fact that she wasn't perfect at everything she tried right away. When Susan started taking driving lessons from her father, she felt that she was "failing miserably!"

Actually, Susan's father complimented her after they went out on her first practice session driving a car. Susan thought her father was just being nice because he was trying to make her feel good. Susan thought, "I stunk at parallel parking. I don't think I'll ever be able to do it. And I forgot to put on my turn signal when I made that left turn in the parking lot. Sometimes I'm just so stupid. How could I do that?"

Do you think Susan felt pride in learning a new skill?

What could Susan have told herself to make herself feel better about taking on this new challenge?

If your fear of failing or anxiety about handling the situation keeps you from enjoying it, you are looking at the challenge as an obstacle. You might want to get the advice of adults or friends on how you can deal with the new opportunity without feeling overwhelmed and stressed out. You can also use the tools that you already read about, such as using calming strategies and helpful self-talk (e.g., "I can have fun even if I don't do things perfectly").

Your Stress Habits

You may know some kids who twirl their hair, bite their nails, or shake their feet under the table. Many habits aren't done for a clear reason. For example, the hair twirlers aren't trying to get rid of straight hair. The nail biters aren't trying to groom themselves, and the people who shake their feet under the table are usually not trying to burn calories!

There are also people who have a habit of always reacting to stress in the exact same way.

Do you have any habits for dealing with obstacles and stress in your life? If so, how do they work? Do they help you to feel more capable and able to deal with the situation? Do they let others know what you need? If so, that's great! If not, here are some strategies you could try:

- Use self-talk to remind yourself that you can deal with some stress on your own.
- Use self-talk to also remind yourself that if you're really upset, you can talk to others to ask for the specific help you need.
- Use the "pebble, rock, or boulder" exercise to figure out how upsetting the situation really is.
- Use calming strategies to relax when you are upset.

Having one way that you usually respond to stress is fine, if it works, as long as it's not your only strategy! The more strategies you have, the more options you will have for responding to stressful situations. When you find yourself stressed, take a deep breath, try to use calming strategies, then think about the most effective way you can respond, even if it's not the way you usually deal with it.

Key Points

- Disappointment doesn't have to overwhelm you.
- You can find creative solutions to problems.
- How you think about new experiences can determine if they end up being fun or if you are too upset to enjoy them.

JOSHUA'S *story*

When Joshua was stressed, he would cry. He cried when his grandfather died, he cried at school when he found out that he forgot his lunch at home, he cried when he found out he wasn't a starter on his basketball team, he cried when he found out he got an A- on his social studies paper, and he cried when his mother didn't have his favorite dessert in the freezer.

There is nothing wrong with crying. People often cry when they are sad, frustrated, overwhelmed, and even angry. But Joshua reacted in the same way when he received an A- as he did when he learned his beloved grandfather had died. When Joshua's uncle pointed this out to him, Joshua admitted, "That's what I do. I cry when I'm upset. Most people don't even pay attention when I cry because I cry so much."

Joshua's uncle suggested that Joshua try to rate his feelings of being "upset" on a scale from 1–10, with 10 being super upset. Then, Joshua's uncle asked him to try to find a way to accurately communicate his feelings and needs to others. If he was only a little upset, he could say "I'm a little sad" or "I'm a little disappointed." However, if he was extremely upset, he could use stronger words, such as "I'm super upset." This way, others could better understand exactly what he is feeling. His habit of crying left people wondering if he was equally upset each time he cried.

Joshua learned that crying had been his habit for dealing with any and all discomfort. After learning to find the right words to describe his emotions to others, he also learned other resiliency strategies, such as changing his "all-or-nothing thinking" (see Chapter Four), and he cried less. He was also much happier.

Have you ever felt like Joshua?

What other strategies could Joshua use to deal with his stress?

Summary

In this chapter you learned that there are creative ways to deal with decision making, you don't have to be defeated just because you are disappointed, and you generally don't have to rush into finding solutions. You also read that people may react to stress in one certain way, just because it has become a habit, and you learned about ways to deal with this. In the next chapter, you will read about ways that you might be able to deal with specific situations that you have some control over.

CHAPTER SEVEN

Having the Power of Change

Have you ever gotten stressed out because you didn't leave enough time to study for a test or you forgot to do something? Most people have! The good news is that these situations are often within your control. They may cause you to be stressed, but you have some power to change them!

You have already read about many ways to deal with stress and obstacles. In the next few chapters, you will figure out how to cope with specific situations. This chapter will focus on how you can handle and bounce back from stressful experiences when you actually have the power to change them. You will learn about how to deal with disappointment in your own actions, being over-scheduled, how to become flexible when plans change, how to set and work toward goals, ways to handle feelings of competition, and what to do when you feel unprepared for handling a situation. But first, take a moment to think about how you deal with stressful situations that are in your control.

If I disappoint myself, I

a) use unhelpful self-talk and get upset

b) try to use helpful self-talk to feel better

c) try to use helpful self-talk and try to learn from the situation

When I am stressed at school, I

a) distract myself by hanging out with friends and trying to forget the stress

b) get nervous or upset, but don't know what to do about it

c) recognize that I'm stressed, and use strategies to feel better, or ask for help to deal with the situation

When I am super busy, I

a) get nervous and end up not giving my total energy to anything

b) try to plan out a schedule, but usually forget some things I should be doing

c) stick to a schedule, so I remember everything I'm supposed to be doing

When my planned schedule has to change, I

a) get very upset and try to avoid having to make the change

b) try to stay calm, but I don't like changes

c) have strategies to help me to make the changes without a lot of stress

If I am in a competition, I

a) get very nervous and hate it

b) am a little nervous, but I remind myself that I don't have to always focus on winning

c) have a bunch of different strategies, including self-talk, to help me get through competitions without a lot of stress

If you answered mostly "a": You are just learning how to handle situations where your actions can make a huge difference. As you read this chapter, you can pick up some useful tips!

If you answered mostly "b": You have some strategies, but could probably benefit from having more tools in your toolbox.

If you answered mostly "c": You have many strategies to help you deal with disappointment, over-scheduling, or other situations that are in your control!

Handling Disappointment After Procrastination

In the last chapter, you read about ways to handle disappointments that can happen when you have to pick between two choices or when things don't go the way you had hoped. But what about the disappointment that comes from being frustrated or upset with your own actions?

You may think, "Why would I disappoint myself?" It may not seem logical. No one sets out to disappoint themselves. Yet, lots of people do this! For example, have you ever waited until the last minute to do a project for school, and then didn't have enough time to do a good job? By waiting until the last minute to work on a project, people don't make a decision to disappoint themselves. In fact, they might not feel like they made any decision at all—they might feel like they were a "victim of the clock" because they ran out of time to do their assignment.

Were you ever a "victim of the clock"? Have you ever procrastinated working on a project until just before the due date? Did you rush to complete the project at the last minute and then run out of time to do it? Did you *decide* to focus on other activities rather than do the work, until there was little time to do the project well? Making a decision to wait until the last minute to work on a project can lead to disappointment if you find that you run out of time.

So, what can you do to avoid being disappointed after you procrastinate? The following tips might help:

- Remind yourself that putting off your work or responsibilities won't make them go away and may only add tension to your life.

- Getting organized and planning when to take care of chores and tasks can help you to deal with them without tons of stress.

- Even if you would rather be doing other activities, find time to fit in the work you *must* do even while doing the things you *want* to do.

- Try not to make excuses (e.g., "I didn't know the test was this week").

If you are upset with how you handled a situation, it is okay to admit your error to trusted others and ask for guidance on how you might have handled it better.

Being Over-Scheduled

Did you know that many kids end up being so busy that they can't enjoy what they are doing because they are stressed and exhausted? You may sign up for a lot of activities so that you don't miss out on anything. However, if you don't have any time to relax, it's hard to keep going from one activity to another without feeling a bit of stress. You might be over-scheduled!

Some people relax while doing activities and don't feel stressed out by having a super busy schedule. Others need scheduled time to relax. Think about yourself. How do you handle being busy every day after school and during the weekends? Do you get moody or irritable because you are tired? Do you have trouble finding time to practice your pitching in baseball, your piano after a lesson, or complete your homework? If so, you might need to take a look at your schedule and see if there's anything you can cut to free up some more time.

You may also find that it's harder to eat well and sleep enough because of your busy schedule. If you don't take care of your body by eating well and getting enough sleep, and you are trying to keep active in lots of activities, you may have an extra hard time being resilient when you face a stressful situation.

Think about what you do every week and see if you can fit in some "me time." This is time that isn't for any specific activity. It's time when you are just hanging with yourself. You may decide to watch TV, go for a jog, enjoy a hobby, or play a videogame. No one else tells you that you need to be somewhere else during this time. It's a chance to unwind and relax. It's a chance to catch up on sleep too, if you need it.

Dealing With Changes

Flexibility means that that you can deal with changes in plans, or quickly rethink how you will deal with a situation when you get new information. Think about a rubber band. A rubber band is flexible: it can twist, bend, and stretch without breaking. Resilient people can change their opinions, deal with new or unexpected experiences, and accept advice from other people that might cause them to rethink how they approach a stressful situation.

Like a rubber band, though, everyone has their "breaking point." If you stretch the rubber band too much, it may break. Similarly, there are limits to what each person can adapt to or deal with easily. Some changes are easy to accept! If your class won't be having math today because the principal planned a surprise activity that you know you will enjoy, you can probably accept this change. However, accepting that someone you love has died or that your long-awaited vacation has to be postponed is much, much harder. It's okay to cry or to be sad, angry, disappointed, or frustrated. Being flexible and resilient doesn't mean you don't have these emotions. It means, though, that you find a way to bounce back or move forward despite having these feelings.

Here are some tips for being flexible, even when times are tough:

- Use self-talk and calming strategies.

- Think about how the person you admire most might handle the situation and think about whether that strategy might work for you.

- Remember that there is not only one way to think—it's okay to change your mind once you learn more information.

- If you struggle with sudden changes in schedules, let your parents and teachers know. Maybe they can agree to give you more advance notice or more time to adjust before the change happens.

- If you get super stressed when you are asked to be flexible, try thinking about whether the actual situation is super serious, or if it's just that your reaction feels super serious.

- If just your reaction is super serious, try telling yourself that you don't like the change of events, but that calming down can help you.

- If the situation is super serious, ask adults to help you get through this difficult time.

Flexibility is not always easy, but you do have some control over how you think about and deal with situations. Some people are resistant to any change. Some people love surprises and are always flexible. Most people are in between these extremes. Being resilient means that you are often able to handle changes and adapt to new situations without a high level of stress. Does this describe you?

ISABELLE'S *story*

Isabelle hated reading directions. She put together a doll house for her little sister just by looking at all the parts and figuring it out. Isabelle said, "I have always done fine without reading directions. Even when I used to take tests, I would see what the questions were and figure out what the teacher wanted to know. I always got good grades. Well, until now. Sixth grade is tricky. I got back two test grades last week that were low, just because I didn't read the directions."

Isabelle explained, "In my vocabulary test, I was supposed to circle the two answers from the list of four choices that could define each word. I thought I was only supposed to find one correct definition. I also messed up a math test because I didn't read that I had to show my work. I got the right answers but didn't get points because I did the work in my head."

Isabelle was angry with her teachers, disappointed with herself, and reacted by telling her parents, "Sixth grade is just stupid. I hate it!"

Do you agree with Isabelle?

What decisions did Isabelle make that resulted in her being disappointed with herself?

What could Isabelle do differently next time?

How Do You Handle Competition?

Competition can be healthy and motivating or it can be stressful and unenjoyable. Gloria, for example, wanted to be one of the best handball players at recess. She loved playing and loved practicing. Even when she lost to someone else, she silently complimented herself on her improvements, and was okay with not winning every time. In this case, competition is a good thing for Gloria.

On the other hand, competition can add stress to your life when it means the experience or game isn't fun because it creates too much tension and discomfort. Competition is also unhelpful if it leads a person to make unhealthy choices in order to win.

ALAN'S *story*

Alan thought about dropping out of the debate club after finding out that he didn't win a medal in the competition that was held at the local community center. He told his teacher, "If I'm not good enough to win the debate, then I don't want to waste my time in the club anymore." Alan used to love debating. He wanted to give up something that he enjoyed doing just because of his difficulty coping with not winning the competition.

What do you think of Alan's plan?

What could Alan tell himself to feel better about continuing in the club?

Even when a person is disappointed or stressed during a competition, there are ways to cope and learn to feel more comfortable. Here are some strategies that could help:

- Use helpful self-talk to remind yourself that it took courage to enter the competition and that you can enjoy the process.

- Use calming strategies so that you can reduce your stress and increase enjoyment in the competition.

- Be careful not to use unhelpful self-talk (e.g., "I didn't win the competition. I'm just not smart! In fact, I must be stupid!").

- Make sure that you are not overgeneralizing. This means that you assume that if you made a mistake in one competition, you'll make it again next time. Or, if you didn't win this time, you won't win next time.

- Speak to members of your support team if you are upset or frustrated.

- Learn from the experience! Try to find something about the experience to motivate you and encourage you to try again.

Did you know that competition between friends has also led to some friendships ending? This will be discussed more in the next chapter, but it shows how important it is to notice and deal with signs of unhealthy or unhelpful competition.

DID YOU KNOW?

There is competition that is helpful and competition that is not. So how can you tell the difference? People sometimes feel stress and discomfort when dealing with competition, especially when they are super competitive individuals. If you find that competition causes you to feel overwhelmed or anxious, try using the coping strategies you already read about or ask someone you trust for help. On the other hand, helpful competition can lead to resilience. If you find that competition helps motivate you to excel, then it can be a positive experience for you!

Ozturk, M.A. & Debelak, C. (2008). Affective benefits from academic competitions for middle school gifted students. *Gifted Child Today, 31*(2), 48–53.

How to Set and Work Toward Realistic Goals

It's easy to sometimes feel stressed or overwhelmed if you feel that the work you have to do is too difficult. Or sometimes your parents' expectations or your own goals might seems too difficult to achieve. It's easy to give up on work or goals if you think it would be impossible to accomplish. That's why it's important to find goals that you can reach successfully, even if it might take time.

Do you set realistic goals for yourself? It is okay to dream about one day becoming president or the mayor of your town. A realistic goal for now might be to read about what's happening in the government or try running for student council at school. It's okay to dream about becoming a famous movie star, but right now you might want to set a reachable goal of trying out for the school play. See how this works? Dreams are important. For now, focus on more immediate goals that you feel confident that you can reach. This way, you can feel the satisfaction and pride of accomplishing them! When faced with the stress of reaching unrealistic goals, you can be resilient by changing them to manageable and realistic short-term ones!

Key Points

- If you disappoint yourself, learn from it instead of getting mad at yourself.

- Being able to deal with unexpected changes in your schedule can help you to be flexible and more resilient!

- Handling competition and setting realistic goals are things you can control and can help you reduce stress and bounce back from difficult situations.

Summary

In this chapter, you learned about how to avoid disappointing yourself, how to handle being over-scheduled, and even how to set goals that you can reach. In addition, you learned about competition and about how being able to adapt to changes in plans can help you become more resilient. Now, it's time to focus on social stress and ways to be resilient when you are dealing with conflicts with your family or friends.

CHAPTER EIGHT

Dealing With Social Conflicts

It's true: other people can cause you stress. Social conflict, or stress between people, can include times when you and a friend or family member have different opinions, when you want to do something different than what your friend wants to do, when you are involved in stressful competition, or when you are being teased or bullied. Some of these stressful situations may be within your control to change. For some, you may not be able to change what is happening, but you can find a way to accept or deal with the situation. If you learn ways to handle these challenges, you can bounce back more easily and become more resilient!

Before reading this chapter, take a minute to reflect on how well you deal with social conflicts and issues already.

When I don't get my way, I

a) get so angry that I have a hard time thinking

b) try to stay calm and convince the other person to change his or her mind

c) stay calm and use self-talk to remind myself that I want to get my way, but I can deal with sometimes letting others get their way or compromising

If I am teased or bullied, I

a) try to ignore it, even when it hurts me

b) tell my parents and sometimes ask for their suggestions, but I make them promise not to tell anyone

c) know when to deal with a situation on my own, when to get suggestions from others, and when to let adults step in

When my friend and I disagree, I

a) start to wonder if I should keep the friendship

b) try to respectfully convince my friend to agree with me

c) accept that my friend can have opinions that aren't always the same as mine

If I'm in a disagreement or conflict with a family member, I

a) don't know how to get past it

b) try to either forget it or get them to agree with me

c) know how to talk it out, share ideas, and then negotiate or compromise when it's necessary and possible

When I'm looking to make new friends, I

a) try to be friends with anyone who is willing to talk to me

b) look for friends who think like I do

c) look for friends who have the same values as I do—like being nice to people—but who don't have to be exactly like me

If you answered mostly "a": You may be struggling to find ways to deal with social conflicts. In this chapter, you will read about some strategies that can help you when you disagree with someone else.

If you answered mostly "b": You have some ways to deal with conflicts, but they may not always help you to get past them. You may pick up some new information in this chapter.

If you answered mostly "c": You already have some great strategies for dealing with social conflicts, but you may find more great tips in the upcoming pages!

Tips for Dealing With Friendship Tensions

It is not unusual for friends to sometimes disagree. Even when friends care about each other and try to respect each other's opinion, sometimes disagreements or even arguments can occur when two people have different views or want to do different things. How do you bounce back and save the friendship when there is a conflict or tension? Here are some tips that have worked for other kids and may work for you too:

❶ Figure out what you think the problem is between the two of you.

❷ Figure out what you want to happen (your goal) so that the conflict is resolved.

❸ Decide if your goal is realistic. Is it fair to your friend?

❹ Determine if the situation is one that you can work to fix, or if you have to just accept certain things about your friend.

❺ Ask yourself what your friend's goal might be.

❻ When you talk to your friend, try using nonjudgmental "I" messages (for example, "I am hurt when…").

❼ Let your friend know that you don't want to end the friendship—you just want to get past the tension.

❽ Ask your friend for his or her view of what's happening. You may be surprised by your friend's response!

❾ When trying to work through the conflict with your friend, try restating what you heard your friend say to make sure you understand him or her correctly before you respond.

❿ Apologize if you realize you hurt your friend's feelings.

Getting past a conflict in your friendship can make you more comfortable dealing with disagreements in the future, and it may even make your friendship closer and stronger.

If you try the strategies above and the disagreement continues, and you aren't comfortable continuing the friendship, talk with trusted adults about whether there is a way to save the friendship or if it is time to end it and perhaps just be acquaintances.

Negotiation and Compromise

You may need additional strategies to handle conflict with friends. Two strategies you might want to try are negotiation and compromise. Negotiation is when you try to solve a problem or disagreement in a way that works for both people that are involved. Compromise means that neither person may get 100 percent of what they want, but they can both accept the solution and move forward.

For example, Jeremy and Nicholas are brothers and both love to sit in the front seat of their family car. They fought a lot about this and both tried to push each other out of the way so that the other brother didn't get into the car's front seat. This plan wasn't working. They talked it out and tried to find a solution to this—that is, they negotiated and found a compromise: neither brother sat in the front seat all the time. They decided that Jeremy would get the front seat on odd numbered days (such as August 9th) but Nicholas would get the seat on even numbered days (such as August 10th).

If you and your friend are fighting over which seats you will get on the school bus each morning, can you think of a way to negotiate and come up with a compromise? When you try to find a solution that works for both of you, remember to:

- Work together. You are looking for solutions, not to force another person to do something that he or she hates or strongly dislikes.

- Say what your goals are, and ask your friend what his or her goals are. Perhaps your goal is to have a window seat, while your friend's goal may be to sit close to another kid who has the window seat in the next row.

- Be flexible when you brainstorm solutions.

- Stick to talking about the problem you are trying to solve, not who won a fight last week or last month.

- Be fair.

Now, take a minute to think about how you might work out the bus seat disagreement. What do you think of these solutions?:

- "My friend and I will switch days sitting by the window."

- "Since my friend doesn't really want the window, just to sit near Sarah (who sits in the window seat in front of us), we can ask Sarah if she would be okay sitting in the aisle seat in front of us. This way, I get the window and my friend gets to be near Sarah in the aisle."

- "I can let my friend know that sometimes I don't mind her talking to Sarah instead of me, even though I'm sitting closer."

- "I can see if I can have the window seat for longer rides on field trips if she gets it during the ride to school each morning."

- "I can be open to solutions that my friend offers."

Be creative! Remember, you want a solution that allows both you and your friend to feel listened to and respected. If your friend broke his leg and needed the aisle seat on the bus because it was hard for him to move into the window seat, you may just let him have the seat after you heard his reasoning, right? You are likely to find that compromise is often appropriate, but sometimes there are good reasons to let other people have their way or vice versa.

You, and your friend, can feel better able to cope with conflicts or disagreements in the future if you find ways to negotiate and compromise now.

While learning to negotiate and compromise can help you to deal with and overcome some obstacles, there are times when you may be asked to compromise when you should not. Whenever you are being pressured to do something unsafe or to do something that you don't want to get involved in, such as teasing or drugs, it's okay to say "no." Knowing when to compromise and when to say "no" can be difficult. Take a moment to think of times when you can compromise and times when you need to stand up for what is right for you.

DID YOU KNOW?

Compromise is such an important concept that it has even been included in research. For example, a study found that people who are able to compromise during times of conflict are looked at more favorably by others and they are better able to make friends! If you take a minute to think about the results of the study, do they make sense to you? Wouldn't you rather be friends with someone who knows how to compromise? Don't you think that other kids would also prefer friends who know how to compromise? It's worthwhile to work on compromising if you have some difficulty with it. Making an effort to be more flexible so you can compromise can help you in your friendships!

Tezer, E. (1999). The functionality of conflict behaviors and the popularity of those who engage in them. *Adolescence, 34*, 409–415.

Controlling a Friendship

Remember reading about the benefits of being flexible in Chapter Seven? Well, flexibility is also important when dealing with friendships and family relationships. Many people would get frustrated with a friend who always had to make the rules and do things his or her way. In other words, kids often don't like other kids who try to always control what they do and what they think! This may seem obvious, yet a lot of people who can't "go with the flow" and be flexible end up trying to control friendships.

If you try to control all situations, that's a lot of pressure on you! Here are some ways to begin to be flexible, let others make plans, and be more comfortable when situations happen that are really out of your control:

- Start going along with some of the plans suggested by friends. See how it goes. You may even feel relieved that you don't always have to control everything.

- Remember that you still can make some decisions.

- Choose to agree to plans that sound safe and fun—you also still have the ability to say "no" if you don't think the plan is safe for you.

LIAM'S *story*

Liam felt pressure from his friends to play a game of "Chicken" with them. This game involved standing on railroad tracks and jumping off of them just before the train came. Liam thought about compromising. He said, "Maybe I should just go with my friends, stand on the tracks, then jump off when I see the train before it even gets close." What do you think of this compromise?

Liam decided that he was being asked to do something that he thought was unsafe and, in his words, "stupid!" He finally told his friends, "I think it's a dumb game. I even heard about these two teenagers who played this game and ended up dead. I'm not interested in that game. I wish you wouldn't do it either." Liam suggested that they try archery or rock climbing at the local gym and they agreed to try those things instead. Liam told his mom, "I think some of my friends didn't want to play the 'Chicken' game either, but didn't know how to get out of it."

What do you think of Liam's suggestion that he and his friends try other activities?

Have you ever been in a similar situation?

Have a plan for when you can't control a situation—for example, when a friend doesn't want to go to the mall with you or your parents are fighting. Hint: Who can you talk to? Can you use your calming techniques? Can you remind yourself that even though these situations may make you feel stressed, you can handle them?

Many people would prefer to do what they want to do all the time. However, these same people value friendships and want to keep their friends. Usually, you can't always be in control and still have a lot of friends who will accept this. Friends may get annoyed or even feel disrespected when they never get to do what they want. By being flexible and giving up some control, you may find that you can develop better friendships!

Dealing With Stressful Competition

In Chapter Seven, you read a little about how to handle competition. Now, let's focus on how competition can affect your friendships. Competition can be fun for you and your friend. It can help to motivate both of you to work hard.

For example, Kenny and his friend Harold had what they called a "friendly competition" over who collected more Most Valuable Player (MVP) baseball cards. Kenny and Harold didn't get mad at each other if they weren't winning this competition. They just kept working to get more MVP cards.

Maggie and Emily, however, didn't end up having a "friendly competition." They competed to see who got higher grades on tests. At first, the friends decided, "Let's see who gets the highest grades this month. Whoever gets higher marks will have the other friend bake her cookies." When the month began, both girls studied hard to get the highest grade. Therefore, it seemed like the competition was motivating them to work hard and study. Guess what happened by the beginning of the second week?

When Emily kept getting slightly higher marks than Maggie, Maggie didn't find the game fun anymore. She didn't want to quit because she had agreed to the competition for the entire month. Instead, she just got annoyed with Emily and started hanging out with other kids. This competition was hurting their friendship.

When competition leads to hurt feelings or a lot of stress in a friendship, then the competition is unhealthy, unhelpful, and stressful.

Are you involved in competition that's really not good for you? Is so, can you think of a creative solution? Stressful competition can be thought of as an obstacle—there are ways around it or to deal with it, but it just takes time to find the right solution to the situation.

Coping With Teasing

Teasing can be confusing, because not all teasing is done to hurt someone's feelings. Some teasing is done when kids feel really comfortable with each other. Sometimes when people are being teased, the "teaser" just thinks he or she is joking around in a friendly way. For example, Nathaniel thought that his best friend, Matt, was teasing him. Matt called him "a nerd" because he liked to do well in school and did an impression of how Nathaniel had nervously asked out a girl. Matt thought these comments were done in a friendly way. However, Nathaniel felt awful.

When Nathaniel yelled at Matt, "Cut it out! I hate it when you tease me!" Matt was surprised and upset. He said, "I was totally kidding. My bad! I am sorry. I had no idea."

Have you ever felt like Nathaniel? Do your friends sometimes joke about something you do or say? It is okay to laugh and appreciate the joke, if you think it's not hurtful to you and it's funny. If you don't like the jokes or labels like "jock" or "nerd," speak up, but remember to share your thoughts in a way that stays respectful of your friends.

Sometimes teasing is not friendly, but it is not always done because a person is "mean" either. If you aren't sure if a friend or acquaintance is purposely trying to hurt you by teasing you, what can you do? If the teasing is upsetting you, can you talk with the other person and let him or her know that you don't like this? Listen to what the other person has to say because you will be able to determine if the teasing was accidental or whether the teasing was meant to hurt you! If the teasing was intentional, you may want to reconsider that friendship.

There are times when teasing is not fixed this quickly. If the teasing is bothering you a lot, or if it is not stopping even when you used some strategies on your own—like speaking up to the person who is teasing you—here are some tips that you might want to try:

- Ignore it. Sometimes a person gets bored teasing someone who doesn't react.
- Hang around with friends who will stick up for you.
- Respond with a quick word or phrase that is not disrespectful, such as "Whatever!"
- Remember not to tease back—that can lead to you getting teased even more.
- Seek out trusted people so that they can offer you suggestions if the teasing continues, or hurts a lot.

ROB'S *story*

Rob was teased a lot in sixth grade. Other kids called him nicknames, like "Robber" and "Roberta." One day, he was super angry about it and tired of being teased. He knew what the problem was: he hated the nicknames. Next, he tried to focus on his goal. At first, Rob thought, "I want to find annoying names to say to other kids." What do you think of this plan?

With help from his parents, Rob decided that his goal would be to have other kids just call him by his real name. Rob wanted to tell them, "You guys are acting like jerks when you call me those names." His parents suggested that he think of a strategy that might help the other kids to want to stop. Rob decided to use an "I" message. He said, "When you call me nicknames, it really annoys me a lot! It's not funny! I really want you to just call me Rob."

Rob went to school the next day and decided to try this "I" message on one of the kids who teased him rarely and who usually seemed pretty nice. The other boy said, "I only call you names because you get on my nerves when you always say you are better at math than me." Rob was shocked by this comment, and replied, "So you are saying that I make you upset with what I'm saying too?"

What do you think happened? Both boys ended up apologizing for upsetting the other person and made a pact. The other boy promised not to call Rob nicknames and Rob promised not to say anything about math grades or abilities. Rob was surprised, the next day, to hear this boy tell other kids to "knock it off, it's not funny anymore," when they tried to call Rob "Roberta." Over time, the nicknames basically stopped and Rob felt relieved.

What do you think about the way Rob handled the situation?

What would you have done, if you were Rob?

Some friends tease each other without it ever leading to hurt feelings. Sometimes teasing can end when the other person realizes that it hurts you. If you feel that you are being teased, use your calming strategies, plan what you want to say or do (that won't hurt the other person or yourself!), perhaps ask an adult for guidance, then try your plan. Imagine how great you can feel if your actions cause you to feel proud and to overcome the teasing!

Bullying and Your Response

Bullying happens when someone who seems to have more power (social or physical) than you acts in a way that is negative toward you on purpose and he or she may even repeat this action again. Bullying can be done face-to-face, behind your back (like someone spreading harmful rumors about you), or even online (cyberbullying).

 If you feel that you are being bullied, you do not have to accept this. You may feel insulted, overwhelmed, depressed, nervous, angry, or uncertain. You may be embarrassed and not want to tell anyone. It is hard to bounce back from insults or physical threats if you believe that you will be insulted again or physically hurt. You may feel hopeless about the situation and believe that you can't do anything to change it.

Resilience does not mean that you have to accept mistreatment and bullying. Resilience means that you recognize when you are being bullied and you figure out whether it's okay to confront the other person. (If a confrontation can put you in danger of serious retaliation, then it's important to ask for help from trusted adults.) Resilience sometimes involves being creative, figuring out how to deal with an awful situation, and knowing that you handled it well. Remember that if you are in danger or the bullying isn't stopping—or you notice that someone else is being bullied—get help from a trusted adult.

Finding the Right Friends for You

Sometimes people wish for "an identical twin, just like me, so we would agree on everything." Identical twins may share identical DNA, but they are still two different people. It's very rare for two people, even identical twins, to agree on *everything!*

So, when searching for a friend who is right for you, rather than looking for someone who agrees with you all the time, you might want to look for someone who:

- ☐ Makes you feel comfortable so you can be yourself.

- ☐ Doesn't try to change you or pressure you to do things you don't want to do.

- ☐ Encourages you to do your best.

- ☐ Appreciates you.

- ☐ Shares common interests or humor with you.

- ☐ Has qualities you appreciate.

- ☐ Makes choices that you like.

- ☐ Is someone with whom you are proud to be seen.

Remember: Having small disagreements with friends sometimes may just mean that you both might want to use the skills that you learned about earlier in this book, such as flexibility, negotiation, and compromise. It doesn't mean the friendship has to be over.

Coping With Family Disagreements

It is natural to have different opinions than other people, whether they are brothers, sisters, parents, or grandparents, or even a spouse when you are older. Brothers and sisters can disagree on just about everything! Parents and children sometimes experience tension when they have different goals. For example, Becca's mom wanted her to go to sleep early on weeknights so that she would be wide awake in school the following day. Becca wanted to stay up later so that she could watch her favorite TV show and Skype with her friends. Becca and her mother often disagreed about her bedtime because they were focused on different goals.

Luckily, the strategies for working through conflicts with friends can usually work with family members as well. If you were Becca, you could listen to your mom, ask your mom to listen to your views, be respectful, and see if this is a situation where you can compromise. At times, your parents are probably going to set certain rules and guidelines that are not open for negotiation, so you need to think about when to continue to discuss and when to accept the situation. Being resilient means that you have strategies for working through situations that can be changed *and* skills for accepting situations that cannot.

Take a moment to think of a time when you and your parents, or siblings, disagreed. How did you work it out? Did you use any of the skills that you read about in this book to help you to work out a family conflict? You might want to write down the skills that you learned (e.g., calm down, think before speaking, be respectful, be flexible, listen to the other person, compromise at times) on a piece of paper so you can refer to them if you ever find yourself in a conflict.

Key Points

- Friendships involve fun times and respect, but also compromise.
- Bullying is never something you need to deal with in silence!
- The right friendship is one where you can be yourself and be proud of your actions when you are with this friend.
- You and your parents may disagree, but those differences of opinion can be worked out so that you can be more comfortable when you are together.

Summary

In this chapter, you read about the importance of being flexible and compromising at times. Ways to deal with teasing and bullying, the risks of being involved in stressful competition, what qualities to look for in friends, and how to deal with family disagreements were all discussed. In the next chapter, you will read about ways to cope with tough times that are beyond your control, such as when your parents get a divorce, and ways to move forward despite the seriousness of these situations.

CHAPTER NINE

Coping With Unchangeable Situations

Sometimes you will have to deal with obstacles and stressful situations that you cannot change or control. You don't have magical powers to make everything just right or keep loved ones happy and healthy. But the good news is that even when you cannot control the situation, you *can* control how you deal with it—and you can learn resiliency skills to help you to bounce back and deal with these tough times more easily.

In this chapter, you will read about some of the major stressful situations that people might have to face in their lives and ways that resilient people have dealt with situations that may seem unimaginable. Remember reading about pebbles, small rocks, large rocks, and boulders in Chapter Three? The situations that are discussed in this chapter could be considered to be boulders by many people. Hopefully, you will never have to face super tough times or major obstacles. However, it's good to know that there are strategies to handle even these stresses.

Before reading on, take a moment to answer the following items and see how you deal with situations that are outside of your control.

When it comes to figuring out which situations I can control and which I cannot, I

a) am always confused about this

b) sometimes know which is which and sometimes am not sure

c) know when I can control a situation and when I can't

When I'm experiencing a really tough time, I

a) don't know if I should ask for help and, if so, whom I should turn to

b) sometimes want to get help from others but I don't know what to say to them

c) have trusted people I can turn to for support to help me to face tough times

When I am faced with a boulder-sized obstacle, I

a) get overwhelmed and think that other people would be able to handle it better

b) become embarrassed that I'm not able to always handle the situation on my own

c) know that even resilient people can feel challenged by boulder-sized obstacles, so I don't get too down on myself if I need help to deal with these times

When I'm experiencing stressful times, I

a) just stay in my room because I am overwhelmed

b) try to do some fun things, but can't often get the motivation to do them

c) know that sticking to my regular routine can help me and distract me when I'm going through tough times

When I'm dealing with a super stressful situation, I

a) don't have any strategies to deal with it

b) use some strategies that calm me down a little bit, but I get mad at myself when I'm still upset

c) use strategies to calm myself down, use self-talk, ask for help, and understand that it's okay to be upset or uncomfortable when experiencing boulder-sized situations, such as the loss of a family member

If you answered mostly "a": You are developing coping skills. Read on to learn some skills for dealing with stressful situations that are outside of your control.

If you answered mostly "b": You have some strategies for coping with serious obstacles and situations that are out of your control, but could benefit from more.

If you answered mostly "c": You have lots of good coping strategies already. Read on to learn even more tools in this chapter.

Facing Major Physical Challenges

A physical disability can certainly create challenges and stress since it affects a person's daily life. Even a person with a less permanent physical injury—such as a broken leg or a strained ankle—can be frustrated, sad, and even angry or resentful.

With physical disabilities or injuries, people may not be able to entirely control what is happening, but they can control how they think about the situation and their self-talk.

Shannon, for example, broke her left ankle right before the championship lacrosse game. There wasn't anything she could do to fix the situation—her ankle needed time to heal. However, she *could* control how she acted and how she managed her emotions. She could be miserable about missing the game or get annoyed with other players because they were going to get to play. If she was angry at her friends just because they were going to play in the lacrosse game, her friends may get upset with her.

Shannon found that using helpful self-talk—for example, "I had a great season and can play again next year!"—and calming strategies allowed her to be less upset and more supportive to her teammates.

Shannon could not change the fact that her ankle was broken, but she could control her disappointment and hurt so that it didn't adversely affect her friendships. She was able to recognize that she contributed to her team's success and that they had a great season!

EVAN'S *story*

When he was very young, Evan was diagnosed with cerebral palsy (CP), a disability that generally can affect movement. He struggled to control his hands and had trouble writing neatly and feeding himself easily. Although many kids with CP are able to walk, Evan was confined to a wheelchair. Evan worked with his physical therapist and occupational therapist to gain strength and control of his body, but he remained in his wheelchair.

Evan told his mother, "I hate being different. I hate not being able to walk like other kids and I hate being stuck in my body." Are his emotions wrong? No. Emotions are just how a person reacts internally to a situation.

Evan's anger began to interfere with his friendships. He didn't want to watch his friends shoot baskets on the basketball court or go to his friend's house to play videogames because he was angry and jealous that his friends don't have CP. He also stopped singing and dropped out of the school's book club because he was too angry to enjoy these experiences.

Evan's school psychologist talked with him, and helped Evan realize that he had lots of control over whether he hung out with his friends, whether he had fun times in his life, and whether he looked at himself as "a kid with CP" or "a smart kid who is popular and has an amazing sense of humor, who happens to also have cerebral palsy." Once he changed his focus, Evan found that he was a lot happier.

Evan was dealing with a very tough situation that he had little control over. How do you think he felt after he changed his focus to what he could control?

What else does Evan have control over?

What other helpful thoughts could Evan tell himself?

If you have an injury or a physical disability, here are some strategies that can help you to move forward and enjoy life despite these struggles:

- Figure out how you feel about the situation. Remember that whatever emotions you have or whatever you are feeling is not wrong.

- Think about whether how your body works is keeping you from focusing on and enjoying fun parts of your life.

- Focus on your abilities. Accept that there may be some things you can't do, but then spend time making a list of all the fun things that you *can* do.

- Try creating a few sentences about who you are—it's a good way to remind yourself that you are not your disability; you are a complicated person with strengths and challenges.

- Tell your parents about activities that you can do and would enjoy, then sign up!

- Talk to your parents about whether a therapist, such as a physical therapist, occupational therapist, speech therapist, or psychologist, could help you to adapt or deal with your physical difficulty.

- Share your goals with the therapists who are helping you.

- Change unhelpful self-talk into helpful self-talk (see Chapter Four).

- Use calming strategies to relax your body and mind when you are too upset to cope with the stress you are experiencing (see Chapter Five).

- Think about how you are treating others. Is anger or sadness keeping you from being a good friend to them?

- Do you have people you can talk to about how you are feeling? If so, do you actually talk to them? If you don't, take a moment to think about people you trust and consider sharing your thoughts with them.

You just read about the fact that there are ways to become resilient and move forward, despite dealing with a major obstacle. Have you tried them all? If not, give them a try! Also, can you come up with some additional strategies that help you to deal with the stress of having a physical problem? What strategies work best for you?

DID YOU KNOW?

Did you know that there are some key factors that can separate out kids who show more resilience or less resilience after a major stress, such as a hurricane? In a study of children who were affected by Hurricane Andrew, researchers found that children who had a support team and had skills for handling strong emotions (e.g., anxiety) were often better equipped to manage this tough time than were children who did not have these skills.

What can we learn from this information? If you are anxious, it's important to share this with others so that you can get the support and help you need to manage this emotion. If you are struggling to find strategies to be calm, happy, and resilient, speak up. The more strategies you have for dealing with stress, the better able you will be to cope with and bounce back from tough times.

La Greca, A. M., Llabre, M.M., Vernberg, E.M., Lai, B., Silverman, W.K., & Prinstein, M.J. (2013). Evaluating children's trajectories of posttraumatic stress and predicting chronic dysfunction. *American Psychological Association 2013 Convention Presentation.*

Facing Major Medical Illnesses

The human body is super complex. It can do amazing things such as jump, run, and help us carry out tasks like touching our nose with our finger (even with our eyes closed), and typing on a keyboard. Sometimes illnesses interfere with how our bodies work. Luckily, there are ways to be resilient and deal with these times of stress.

Self-talk can be extremely powerful when a person has to find ways to cope with boulder-sized challenges. An important point to think about, at these times, is the language we use in our self-talk. Self-talk could help people to focus on the positive and things that are within their control, such as "I may have diabetes, and I sometimes have to do things my friends don't have to do, like take insulin and check my sugar levels, but I also can do lots of things that my friends do!"

When dealing with a medical problem, calming strategies can be a great tool for dealing with anxiety or being overwhelmed. It is not unusual for a person to

MITCHELL'S *story*

When Mitchell found out that he had cancer, he had a choice about how he viewed this enormous challenge. At first, Mitchell was angry. He told his doctor, "Why couldn't this have happened to someone else? Why me? I can't deal with this!"

Mitchell's reactions and comments were not unusual. But his doctor suggested that he talk with the social worker in the hospital to find ways to cope with the news that he has cancer. Mitchell's social worker talked to him about "I can't" and "I can" thoughts. After he had several appointments with the social worker, Mitchell told his grandfather, "I hate this cancer. I hate the treatment. I hate missing out on the regular stuff other kids are doing when I'm not feeling good. But, I'm trying to focus on what I can do, so that I don't forget that. My social worker told me that if I only focus on what I can't do, I may feel even more depressed and overwhelmed. I think that's true. Sometimes I feel like I can't do stuff so I talk to my parents and that helps. But I always try to also focus on what I can do. It helps."

Mitchell came up with things that he says to himself when he gets scared about his illness. Here is his self-talk: "I don't want to die. I'm going to do everything I'm supposed to so I get better. My doctors say I have a good chance of beating this cancer enemy. I have good doctors, my parents are always there for me, and I just need to go through the treatments."

Mitchell was more in control of his illness when he knew exactly what was going on with his cancer and what treatment he needed. He also tried to continue in school on most days. Mitchell even figured out how to speak with his doctors about not having treatment the week of his end-of-the-year dance at school. He was trying to bounce back from the despair he had originally felt. He said, "I can try to make the best of this lousy situation" rather than saying that he couldn't handle it.

What do you think you would have done if you were Mitchell?

What else could Mitchell do to help himself to be less stressed?

experience anxiety about what the diagnosis means, what the treatment might include, and what the prognosis will be. By calming down, it is easier to think about the situation, what questions you have, and whom you can turn to for answers. Once you are calmer, you will also likely find that it is easier to find solutions to some situations that are within your control, such as how to keep in touch with friends even though you are in the hospital.

Dealing With Moving

You may wonder what moving is doing in the same chapter as stress from physical disabilities, injuries, and illnesses. Actually, moving can also create strong emotions and challenges. It may seem like a big adjustment in your life that you probably have little or no control over. On a scale of 1–10, with 10 being the most difficult, do you think that moving is super stressful and ranks as a 10? If so, you might need some strategies to help you to deal with your strong emotions.

If you have already overcome an obstacle such as moving, you may have more confidence that you can deal with it again. If you ever find out that you have to move, here are some coping strategies you can use to deal with your stress:

❶ Use calming strategies first, so that you can focus on helpful self-talk or problem-solving strategies.

❷ Think about whether what you are saying to yourself is true or not. For example, you may think that your life is over, but it's really not.

❸ Describe your emotions. Learning how to categorize your emotions and thoughts, and how to share them with others, can help you and others better understand what you are experiencing.

❹ Make a "pro/con" list for moving—the reasons you don't want to move (cons) and the reasons you might enjoy it (pros).

❺ For each "con," try to think of a way around it. For example, if you don't want to lose your friends, figure out ways to keep in touch with them.

JUANITA'S *story*

Juanita had to move because her father's company moved to another state. When Juanita learned that they had to move, she was devastated. Juanita told her sister, "My life is over! I can't leave my friends. I can't start over!"

Juanita's sister said that she was sad about leaving friends, too, but shared some of the things she thought might be exciting about the move, like meeting new people and making new friends. Juanita and her sister brainstormed some ideas to help them to get comfortable with the idea of moving. They decided to try to visit their new school soon, so they could get to know some kids before they move. They also practiced self-talk ("This is an adventure!" and "We can still keep in contact with old friends!") and used this when they felt particularly down about the move.

Juanita still hated the idea of moving but understood that she couldn't change the situation. She felt that she could bounce back from her despair once she calmed down and focused on what she could control, like getting to meet kids before the actual moving date.

Have you ever had to move? If so, did you feel like Juanita?

What else could Juanita do to get more comfortable with the idea of moving?

❻ For each "pro," think of how you can make it happen. For example, if you want to make new friends at your new school, you could research clubs and activities you could join at your new school.

❼ Remember that you are not alone! You can talk about your emotions with your parents or friends. If you know anyone who has moved, you could ask them how they dealt with the transition.

Resilience does not mean that you are always comfortable dealing with obstacles or new experiences. The resilient person is confident that there are people who can be supportive and strategies that can help. The resilient person knows that there are ways to move forward despite these stressful times.

When Someone You Love Dies

If someone important in your life dies, it can be devastating. Not having this person in your life can change plans that you may have had together and dreams of sharing more good times. Even adults struggle with how to cope when a loved one dies.

It's easy to say, "Accept that it happened and bounce back," to people who have lost a family member, another important person in their life, or even a pet. However, this is probably not realistic. Even though they know that the person has died, they may feel numb and not understand why the loss doesn't seem real. This can confuse and scare some kids even though it's entirely normal as a first reaction. In fact, this numbness is kind of a protection—it may keep you from feeling all your emotions at once.

You may also be angry about the fact that the person died and sad about the loss. If the person who died was your parent, you may find that your daily schedule and how it feels to be in your home has changed. If the person was a trusted adult you often went to for guidance, you may feel confused about whom to turn to now that you need so much support.

Accepting that your loved one has died will take time. Acceptance doesn't mean that you like this situation or have to forget about the person. Rather it means that you know that you can't do anything to change it, so you'll try to adjust to it. Don't worry about accepting the death in the first week, month, or even months. It's a process. Even accepting that you couldn't do anything to change the fact that your loved one died can take time.

Here are some strategies for dealing with this major stress:

- Accept your emotions. There are no "right" emotions at this time in your life.

- Know that it's even okay to be angry at the person who died, because that person is no longer there for you.

- If it helps, try writing in a journal or copying pictures into a book about the person so that you have a permanent book about him or her. This strategy can even be helpful if you want to remember a close family pet.

- Don't ignore your emotions. Pretending that you are fine and that nothing is bothering you may deprive you of getting support that you might need. Let people know you would accept their caring and concern.

- Focus on positive memories. If you argued with this person recently, it's not helpful to focus on this. Loved ones sometimes argue. Focus on the love you shared, even if it wasn't directly spoken about.

- Try to return to some of your regular schedule and activities as soon as you can, so that you can experience some things that are familiar and comforting.

- Talk, talk, talk to people who are able to listen and support you. Some kids, however, may be too overwhelmed themselves to listen to your grief, even though they care about you.

- Brainstorm with supportive adults to find a plan for how you can deal with powerful emotions while at school.

People deal with the loss of a loved one in their own way. There is no one right way to grieve. However, if you find that you are overwhelmed and distraught, remember that there are still people in your life that can be part of your support team. Give them a chance to offer support. Give yourself a chance to accept this support.

When Parents Fight or Divorce

If you find that your parents are constantly arguing and keeping you from the calm home that you remember or dreamed of, this can be very stressful. Some kids wish their parents would get a divorce rather than fight. Other kids hope that the parents fight until they work out their differences because they don't want their parents to separate and divorce.

The reality is that parents will do what parents will do. That means that you are a spectator. You can watch, you can distract them at times, or you can try to "fix" things by trying never to cause problems. No matter what you do, however, your parents may still fight. This is an adult problem that has nothing to do with you, and it's not your fault. They may still divorce.

When dealing with these parental conflicts, some kids aren't sure how to react or whom to talk to.

If your parents are arguing, separating, or divorcing, here are some tips you can use to help you to deal with the stress:

- Remind yourself that you didn't cause your parents' problems and you can't solve them either.
- Tell your parents in a calm and respectful way that their fighting upsets you.
- Try to block out their yelling by listening to music in your room.
- Finish your homework at school where you can concentrate better.
- Let your parents know that you need to talk to someone outside of the home about the stress that their arguing or the divorce is having on you. Perhaps your parents and you can pick the person to speak with—someone who doesn't take sides, such as a guidance counselor or a psychologist.
- Remind yourself that divorce doesn't mean that you are divorced from either parent. Can you tell yourself that your parents both love you even if they don't get along with each other?

If your parents ever start doing dangerous behaviors that could hurt someone, you should think about whether it's time to call 911 so that everyone is safe. If you aren't sure if it's dangerous or if you fear that it will become dangerous, talk to a trusted adult who can help you sort it out and be a support to you.

Dealing With Other Disappointments

There are many other situations that are not boulder-sized obstacles, but still can lead to strong disappointment. Lots of people struggle to figure out when to accept a tough situation and when to work super hard to change it.

There are many situations that may upset you but that are out of your control. For instance, imagine that you worked hard on your science project but didn't win the science competition. You can't change the fact that you didn't win first place in this competition. You can just change how you think about it and react to it. Here are two examples of ways that a person might react:

❶ Brent (whom you first read about in Chapter Six) worked hard on his science project. He thought he did a great job and believed that he should and would win first place in the competition. When he found out that he came in third, he grabbed his project, told his dad to bring him home immediately, and he threw his project onto the floor as soon as he walked into his home. He then ran to his room yelling, "I hate the judges. I hate Tommy for taking *my* first place trophy." A few minutes later, he started yelling, "I'm so stupid. I can't believe I thought I could win. I'm never trying anything like that again."

❷ Phillip also put a lot of time into his science project, but didn't make it into the top three winners. He told his best friend, "I really wanted to win. Oh well, maybe next year. Did you see the winner's experiment? That was cool!"

Brent and Phillip were both students in the same school, at the same science competition. Both students put a lot of time and energy into their science projects—they were in control of these factors. However, after they learned that they did not win the competition, their reactions were quite different.

Phillip felt that he had fun and focused on the fact that he tried and that he learned about other experiments. Brent focused on his anger at others and at his "failure" and decided that he was not able to succeed in the future. Phillip used positive self-talk, while Brent did not. Phillip had fun, while Brent did not. Phillip was resilient, while Brent was not.

Resilience does not prevent disappointment. As Phillip admitted, he "really wanted to win," yet he was able to still enjoy the experience. Resilient people recognize and accept their feelings and find ways to deal with times of disappointment and stress.

Key Points

⟳ No matter how hard you try, some situations are not in your control to change.

⟳ When facing a major stress, it's okay to admit that you need support.

⟳ Continuing some of your regular activities can help you to focus on the part of your life that remains the same, even while you are facing incredible stress.

Summary

In this chapter, you read about the importance of knowing that there are some very painful situations that you can't control, but there are ways to try to deal with them. Super tough situations, such as having a physical disability or a major medical illness, learning you are moving away from your school and current home, dealing with parents who are arguing or divorcing, and coping with the death of a loved one were discussed. In addition, this chapter explored ways to deal with everyday disappointments when you can't change the cause of your disappointment. In the next chapter, you will get a chance to think about when you should handle situations on your own, when you should get advice from others, and when you should ask others to step in and help out.

CHAPTER TEN

Building a Support Team

No one is totally independent. Do your parents grow all the food that you eat or do they rely on others to supply some of the food to them at the grocery store? When your teacher goes on vacation, does she fly her own airplane or does she rely on a pilot? The truth is that everyone needs help from others sometimes! It is actually a sign of maturity to know when you can handle a situation on your own and when you need to ask for help or advice. You do not need to be 100 percent independent in order to truly be resilient.

In this chapter, you will read about independence, specifically, when you should handle a situation entirely on your own and when to ask for guidance. You'll also read about when it's a good idea to ask another person to help you deal with a situation and tips on who that person might be. Before you start, take a moment to decide whether you rely on others or act independently in situations.

When stuck with a difficult situation, I

a) usually don't handle it on my own

b) sometimes know I should be able to handle it, but don't know what to do

c) know which situations I can handle on my own and have strategies for dealing with them

When I am faced with a challenging situation, I

a) don't usually ask for guidance from others

b) sometimes ask for guidance, but think it's a sign of weakness

c) am comfortable asking for suggestions from others when I just need another opinion or a few ideas on how to deal with the stress

At times, when a situation is serious or very uncomfortable, I

a) usually refuse to let others help me out, since I like being independent

b) sometimes let my parents or teachers get involved, but I am embarrassed to ask

c) know that it's a sign of maturity to ask for help when a situation is serious or my strategies haven't worked and I'm super uncomfortable

If I do decide to seek help from someone else, I

a) wouldn't even know whom to ask

b) always ask my parents

c) have a support team and ask the person who might be best suited to help. It could be my parents, brother or sister, teacher, or another person I trust

If I decide to talk with my parents about a stressful situation, I

a) expect them to take care of the problem for me

b) want them to tell me what I need to do so that I can do it

c) know when I just want suggestions and when I need them to step in and handle the situation for or with me

If you answered mostly "a": You are just beginning to learn when to rely entirely on yourself, when to ask for guidance, and when it's time to have another person help out. This knowledge is important as you work to become resilient.

If you answered mostly "b": You have some skills for deciding when to ask for help and when to rely on yourself. However, you may learn some additional skills as you read the rest of this chapter.

If you answered mostly "c": You have a variety of resiliency skills and a nice balance between relying on yourself and turning to others. No matter whether you answered "a," "b," or "c," it's always great to be open to learning new skills and ways to bounce back from tough times!

Getting Advice and Guidance

You probably handle many situations on your own every day. You may be great at picking out your outfits for school, doing your math homework, or remembering to do your chores. It's a great time to consider relying entirely on yourself especially when you think that you are prepared, can confidently deal with the expectations, and have the skills to do it.

Solving difficult situations on your own may help you to gain confidence so that you can overcome adversity. However, it is equally as important to know when to seek advice from others and when to let others step in and help.

Seeking advice or guidance doesn't necessarily mean you want someone else to handle the situation for you. You may still handle the situation on your own after asking for suggestions. If so, just let the people you are talking to know that you a seeking suggestions but would like to handle the challenge on your own. Otherwise, they may think that you are asking them to solve the problem for you. For example, you may ask a friend for suggestions on how to find out if a kid likes you. Instead, your friend might just ask the kid directly when all you wanted was tips on what you can do to find out. So it's good to be clear about exactly what you are seeking!

Time for Another Person to Help

If you are being seriously mistreated or are put in a dangerous situation, it's time to seek help immediately. You must speak to others and seek their support even if you are a very capable young person.

RAMON'S *story*

Ramon thought that he was a pretty independent seventh grader. He set his alarm on his iPhone each night to wake him up at the right time in the morning, he got ready for school, made sure to have a quick and healthy breakfast, and was always ready before the school bus arrived. He also did his chores and his homework on his own without being reminded by his parents. Once after an unusually busy family weekend, Ramon needed to finish reading the last fifteen pages of a book before Monday morning. He knew that he was too tired to concentrate on the book. So he asked his mother if she would read the book to him, and he could just focus and listen rather than trying to read and understand the book. His mom agreed to this plan.

What do you think of Ramon's plan?

Do you still consider Ramon an independent and self-reliant person?

Do you think that Ramon knew that recognizing when you need help is a sign of resilience and maturity?

If the situation isn't super serious and you are not being bullied, do you think that it's okay to ask for help? Of course it is okay! If you are trying to manage or cope with a new situation or are super stressed out, just ask! However, just remember that sometimes you might need to take a chance and figure out things on your own. If you always rely on others, you may be depriving yourself of the opportunity to gain knowledge and confidence so that you can cope on your own. You need to balance relying on others and slowly relying on yourself more and more.

If you do ask for help, figure out what help you need (or want). Be very specific when you talk to another person so that he or she knows what support you are looking for. If you know that others have managed to handle an obstacle or challenge in the past and you want their guidance, it's okay to ask. You can learn some valuable information from others!

Sometimes, it's just helpful to ask an adult for more information so that you can better understand a situation. For example, Roy told his father, "Tell the coach to put me on the travel soccer team!" Instead, Roy could have asked his parents for suggestions on how he could approach his coach to ask why he wasn't on the travel team and what he might do to make the team next time around. Roy would gain the satisfaction of having had the conversation on his own even if it didn't change the fact the he wasn't on the travel team.

Remember that adults can sometimes love you enough *not* to fix every stress. It may be their way of helping you to learn that you are ready to handle some tough times without them intervening.

Still you may want your parents or other people to fix situations that you think are uncomfortable or wrong. It can be difficult to deal with disappointments on your own.

So, when is it time for parents to step in and directly help out? Here are a few tips:

- If you *need* rather than just *want* something (such as postponing a test because you are attending a wedding out of town), but you weren't successful in handling the situation, ask an adult to help out.
- If you are in danger or being mistreated, speak up!
- If you are really stuck and need help, seek guidance from an adult, especially when you know that person has successfully managed a similar obstacle in the past or has specific suggestions relating to the situation.

Everyone has to balance relying on others and relying on themselves. If you know that you now have the strategies to cope with some stressful situations and you are not in any danger, can you come up with a way that you want to respond?

Check with your parents or other trusted adults to see if they think that your plan can work. Be open to learning from them, but also try to be open to gradually handling more tough times independently.

DID YOU KNOW?

Do you think that students in classrooms are more likely to ask for help when they are confident in their general academic skills or when they are not? A study actually found that when students doubt their abilities to succeed in school, they are less likely to ask for help. If students don't seek help when they need it, they may not do as well as if they were comfortable seeking guidance. If the students felt that a particular classroom environment stressed competition, those who doubted their skills were even *less* likely to ask for help.

If you find that you are hesitant to ask for help, either because you doubt your abilities in school or you feel that the class environment stresses competition, remember that asking for help can be a very wise action and can help you to overcome the confusion or academic challenge you are facing!

Ryan, A.M., Gheen, M.H., & Midgley, C. (1998). Why do some students avoid asking for help? An examination of the interplay among students' academic efficacy, teachers' social-emotional role, and the classroom goal structure. *Journal of Educational Psychology. 90*(3), 528–535.

Whom Do You Turn to?

Whom do you turn to when faced with a challenging situation and want to seek help? Do you have a team of supporters you can rely on and turn to? Your support team may include lots of people such as your parents, siblings, other relatives, teachers, religious leader, guidance counselor, psychologist, social worker, and even friends. Perhaps certain people would be more helpful to you in one situation and others might be better able to guide you at other times. Take a moment to read some other kids' accounts of stressful situations and think about whom you would turn to for help if you were in the same situation:

- "I'm having a hard time figuring out how to match verbs and nouns in my Spanish class. It's so confusing."

- "I'm switching from elementary school to the middle school next year. I don't know my way around that building."

- "My friend asked me to play a game with her at recess. I said no because I don't know how to play it."
- "Sometimes I need help making friends. What should I do?"

What did you answer? While you can certainly touch base with your parents for guidance, you may want other people to support you in specific situations too. For instance, for the student having trouble in a certain class, the teacher is a great resource. The student who is concerned about not knowing how to get around middle school could talk to an older brother or sister and ask for a virtual (or actual) tour. The student who doesn't know how to play a game at recess could ask her friend to explain the rules.

If you have a serious worry or concern, such as making friends, your parents may be able to guide and advise you. When obstacles cause you a lot of stress, there are also professionals (such as psychologists, school counselors, psychiatrists, and social workers) who are trained to help people overcome or deal with these situations. Your parents can probably help you find one of these professionals, after talking with your guidance counselor, pediatrician, or others who are knowledgeable and can make a referral.

Key Points

- The capable person knows when to rely on oneself and when to get help from others.
- It's helpful to know who the best person is to advise you on how to deal with situations when you are stressed or overwhelmed.
- Having lots of people on your support team lets you have lots of choices for whom to ask for help!

Summary

In this chapter, you read about the importance of knowing when you can handle situations on your own, when it's important to ask for guidance, knowing when to ask others to step in and help out, and how to figure out who to turn to for support to help you to deal with a particular situation.

CONCLUSION

Don't Stop! Your Resiliency Journey Continues

You have learned many ways to deal with stress and difficult times in your life. As you grow and face new experiences and challenges, you may want to refer back to the information in this book to find the coping strategies that work best for you.

Here are a few reminders that you can use as you become more resilient:

- Life can be less stressful if you are confident and resilient!
- Knowing what causes you stress and how you react to stress can allow you to prepare for and deal with those times.
- Emotions aren't good or bad, they just help us to understand ourselves, our wants, and our needs.
- Helpful self-talk is an important strategy to use as you become resilient.
- Once you are calm, you can think more clearly about coping strategies.
- Disappointments, decisions, and other common sources of stress don't have to overwhelm you.
- Some stressful situations are actually under your control and you can learn resiliency skills to deal with them.
- Friendships involve respect and fun, but also compromise.

- Some painful situations may be out of your control, but there are ways to try to cope with or adjust to them.

- It's important to rely on yourself sometimes, but it's also okay to ask for help or guidance at other times.

Congratulations! By reading this book, you've taken the first step toward becoming resilient. Now, the next time you are facing an obstacle or a stressful situation, try out your new skills! If you are more resilient today than yesterday, then you are moving in the right direction. Enjoy the journey toward becoming a more resilient person!

About the Author

Wendy L. Moss, PhD, ABPP, FAASP, has her doctorate in clinical psychology, is a licensed psychologist, and has a certification in school psychology. Dr. Moss has practiced in the field of psychology for over 30 years and has worked in hospital, residential, private practice, clinic, and school settings. She has the distinction of being recognized as a diplomate in school psychology by the American Board of Professional Psychology for her advanced level of competence in the field of school psychology. Dr. Moss has been appointed as a fellow in the American Academy of School Psychology.

In addition, she is the author of *Being Me: A Kid's Guide to Boosting Confidence and Self-Esteem* and *Children Don't Come With an Instruction Manual: A Teacher's Guide to Problems That Affect Learners;* coauthor, with Donald A. Moses, MD, of *The Tween Book: A Growing-Up Guide for the Changing You;* coauthor, with Robin A. DeLuca-Acconi, LCSW, of *School Made Easier: A Kid's Guide to Study Strategies and Anxiety-Busting Tools;* coauthor, with Susan A. Taddonio, DPT, of *The Survival Guide For Kids With Physical Disabilities & Challenges;* and has written several articles.

About Magination Press

Magination Press is an imprint of the American Psychological Association, the largest scientific and professional organization representing psychologists in the United States and the largest association of psychologists worldwide.